YOU CAN

*A Collection of Brief Talks on the most
Important Topic in the World—Your Success*

INCLUDES QUOTES FROM
NAPOLEON HILL AND OTHERS

BY GEORGE MATTHEW ADAMS

"The King is the man who can'
—Carlyle

Compiled with Commentary
by

Don M. Green
Executive Director

A Publication of
THE NAPOLEON HILL FOUNDATION

Revised and Edited by
Don M. Green, Executive Director
The Napoleon Hill Foundation

Published by:
    The Napoleon Hill Foundation
    P. O. Box 1277
    Wise, Virginia 24293

    Website: www.naphill.org
    email: napoleonhill@uvawise.edu

Distributed by:
    Executive Books
    206 W. Allen Street
    Mechanicsburg, PA 17055

    Telephone: 800-233-2665
    Website: www.executivebooks.com

ISBN: 0-937539-46-5

CONTENTS

PREFACE

Webster's Classic Reference Dictionary defines the word *morsel* as a small piece or quantity of food. Many morsels of food for thought are contained throughout this little book.

Information taken in small amounts can lead to positive habits. Good habits—in some ways, success is in itself entirely a matter of habit—habits both of thought and of action.

History of the biographies of great men has shown that the reading of books has been critical to their growth.

W. Clement Stone borrowed one hundred dollars and started an insurance business that accumulated a net worth of several hundred million dollars. As a young boy, he read Horatio Alger books and they had a tremendous effect on his mental outlook on life.

Young Abe Lincoln walked several miles to borrow books and read by the light of a fireplace. Lincoln's education came mostly from books that he was able to borrow.

Little wonder that our third President, Thomas Jefferson once remarked, "I could not live without books."

Read this small book and watch for little bits of information that will assist you on your road to success.

Don M. Green
Executive Director
Napoleon Hill Foundation

❖❖❖❖

The thing always happens that you really believe in; and the belief in a thing makes it happen.

—Frank Lloyd Wright, 1867-1959

To be successful in any sort of endeavor, you must have a definite goal toward which to work. You must have definite plans for attaining this goal. Nothing is ever accomplished that is worthwhile without a definite plan of procedure that is systematically and continuously followed day by day.

—Napoleon Hill, 1883-1970

You will find it easier to be successful if you first know what you want. Next you must plan to take action to get started. You will not be likely to know all the answers when you start but you must not let that prevent you from beginning your success journey.

—Don M. Green, Executive Director
Napoleon Hill Foundation

❖❖❖❖

YOU CAN

YOU CAN make of yourself anything the germ of which lives within you. But to realize your full possibilities—to Dominate and Achieve—you must have High Aims, Ideals and Ambitions—all linked to an Iron Will. You yourself determine the height to which you shall Climb. Have you the Summit in view? All right—

Then Start for it.

YOU CAN take command of yourself at any moment you desire to do so. You can make of yourself a towering figure in the work of the world. No one owns you. One hundred per cent of the Stock in your personal Corporation belongs to you. The little People of Destruction that whine at your door, whine at the door of every forceful man. You can make them mere Pygmies in their Power over your Future. Are you doing this Now? Well—

Then Keep it up!

YOU CAN get Smiles and Cheer and Continued Youth—simply by sticking to your own craft and running your own pilot wheel with "Your Best" as the Place of Port. Results will take care of themselves. Never mind the Sneers, the Criticisms, the Misjudgments of others. Time will fade them all away from you if your Accumulated Strength of Character has taught you how to Wait. Today is Yesterday's plans put into action. Tomorrow begins Today. Your Worth to yourself and the World is measured by what you contribute each day in Usefulness. Success is the Sum of the Days.

Then Do Today.

YOU CAN make Success sure by Work, Sacrifice, Enthusiasm, Unselfishness and Self-control. You are the Master of your own Destiny. Take personal command of yourself Today.

YOU CAN!

❖❖❖❖

The fragrance always stays in the hand that gives the rose.

—Hada Bejar

A cornerstone of the Think and Grow Rich Philosophy is that the more you give, the more you get. In everything you do—for your customers, your associates, your employees, your family—practice doing just a little more than is expected. You'll stand out because there's no traffic jam on the extra mile, and you'll discover that service to others is one of life's greatest riches.

—Napoleon Hill, 1883-1970

One of the principles of success is sowing and reaping. For some reason many people seem to be waiting on their ship to come in rather than swimming out to meet it; therefore, they never really understand the success principles.

It is not possible to carry one to success but we can assist others by helping them to help themselves.

—Don M. Green, Executive Director
Napoleon Hill Foundation

❖❖❖❖

50-50

No man in all this world ever rightfully Gets more than he Gives. And if he does he is just a plain Thief—a discredit first to Himself, then to everybody else. The Equal Division is always the Just Division—half to you and half to him. In other words, on the basis—50-50.

Be glad to Give as much as you Take.

You who are an Employee, are you Sure you are giving in Service as much as you are taking in Money, Experience, Inspiration and Training from your Employer? Right now, take invoice. Do the results look like—50-50? If not, start this plan into action—

Be glad to Give as much as you Take.

This plan of 50-50—rightly interpreted, means death to Whiners, to the Disgruntled, and to the Assassinators of Success. They can't live in the atmosphere of it. The Air is too Invigorating.

Be glad to Give as much as you Take.

Every dispute in this World is traceable to the lack of the 50-50 principle. The broken-up Homes, the disintegrated Businesses, the abandoned Friendships, the wasteful Armies of the World. There is need of this principle in every phase of Life. But never will it become a rule of every-day Action until YOU, in your place, begin to apply—50-50.

Be glad to Give as much as you Take.

❖❖❖❖

Silence has one major advantage: it gives no one a clue as to what your next move will be.

—Napoleon Hill, 1883-1970

*Consider adopting the habit of the **Silent Hour** when you will be still and listen for that small still voice that speaks from within, thus discovering the greatest of all powers—Creative Vision, the one power that can shift you from the failure side of the River of Life over to the success side.*

During your silent hour you will be alone, alone with yourself and God. This is one hour you cannot share with any other. You must go into the silence alone, of your own free will and accord. After you get there, you must speak for yourself. No one can speak for you and nothing will happen—save only that which you inspire by the use of your own initiative. Also, nothing of great importance may happen to you outside of your silent hour except that which you inspire by your own Personal Initiative, and Creative Vision inspires the development of Personal Initiative.

—Napoleon Hill, 1883-1970

❖❖❖❖

Silence

Yes, Silence is many times Golden. You know that. But try to realize it more strongly. For the Silent Man is usually the Thinking Man and the Silent Worker is the Get-Things-Done Worker. But best of all, Silence as a rule of daily life Conduct makes you Big and Powerful.

Don't talk Back.

The World's great Doers have all been Men and Women of few words—Napoleon, Cromwell, Washington, Grant, Lincoln, Marshall Field—Edison. These men didn't have time for disputes, wrangles—revenges.

Don't talk Back.

The World is coming to the Idea of Silence—fewer Words, more Deed-doing. It is the big Law of Nature. It is becoming the great Law of Business. For Silence can't be answered. There is nothing to answer.

Don't talk Back.

Look around you. You admire the Silent people—those who mind their own business and Build. You know the names of the Useful men of your town. You can't waste their time—you can't get them "mad." You can't steal anything from them. Their Silence is their Wealth and every time they walk along the streets they speak volumes. Add another motto to those you may already have. Make it this—Silence.

Don't talk Back.

❖❖❖❖

It is impossible for a man to be cheated by anyone but himself.

—Ralph Waldo Emerson, 1803-1882

You can tell the character of every man when you see how he receives praise.

—Lucius Annaeus Seneca, 4B.C.-65A.D.

The ability to create and maintain a good impression of yourself in the minds of other people smoothes over many of the bumps in the road to success. It can also mean the difference between inspiring antagonism or cooperation in people, whether you have just met them or have known them for years.

—Napoleon Hill, 1883-1970

❖❖❖❖

CHARACTER

Character is the sum total, worth while, of what a man has after he has won all and the sole thing he has left after he has lost all.

Character is Power.

J. Pierpont Morgan, the greatest single power in Finance in all the world, at the time of his death, once stated under oath, that "Character is the only gauge of a man, or the only rule by which he can be gauged in business, and that physical assets are therefore of secondary importance."

Character is Power.

The walls of Character that a man builds will withstand the most merciless assaults that any man can direct at them. A man's or a woman's good Character is absolutely unassailable. Reputation may be besmirched—but not Character. For Reputation is what people may say a man is, but Character is what he really is.

Character is Power.

Character is greater than talent, genius, fame, money, friends—there is nothing to compare with it. A man may have all these and yet remain comparatively useless—be unhappy—and die a bankrupt in Soul. But—Character pays out endless Dividends, molds a man into a mighty Deed-doer, and builds for him a deathless Name.

Character is Power.

Character is Power in Business, in the Home, on the Street—everywhere. And it's free for the asking to the man willing to be kind, honest, square, broad, generous, loyal, fearless—Big! Stamp your Character deeper on people today and make it rule your work. Let it lead you on. But fight every hour to make it stronger. For—

Character is Power.

❖❖❖❖

The greatest mistake you can make in life is to continually fear you will make one.

—Elbert Hubbard, 1856-1915

If the first plan which you adopt does not work successfully, replace it with a new plan; if this new plan fails to work, replace it in turn with still another, and so on, until you find a plan which does work. Right here is the point at which the majority of men meet with failure, because of their lack of persistence in creating new plans to take the place of those which fail.

—Napoleon Hill, 1883-1970

Learning from our mistakes is simply the way one views what has taken place. Results that are not the ones anticipated can be a reason to quit or the obstacle can be counted as a stepping stone. The acceptance of a mistake as a lesson can be used to urge one forward.

—Don M. Green, Executive Director
Napoleon Hill Foundation

❖❖❖❖

MISTAKES

Study your Mistakes.

There are two kinds of Mistakes. Those that happen from ordinary human mis-thinking and those that come from carelessness and petty un-thinking.

Study your Mistakes.

No one ever gets too big to make Mistakes. The secret is that the big man is greater than his Mistakes, because he rises right out of them and passes beyond them.

After one of Henry Ward Beecher's sermons in Plymouth Church, Brooklyn, a young man came up to him and said: "Mr. Beecher, did you know that you made a grammatical error in your sermon this morning?"

"A grammatical error," answered Beecher, "I'll bet my hat that I made forty of them."

Half of the power of the forceful man springs out of his Mistakes of one sort or another. They help to keep him human.

Study your Mistakes.

But the Mistakes that tear away the power of a man, weaken him, and make him flabby, are the stupid, the reckless Mistakes. The Clerk who forgets, the Stenographer that doesn't care, the Worker who neglects—these are the ones whose life blood and vitality is sapped and sucked away into failure.

Study your Mistakes.

One of the great things of each day for you is to do your best—unmindful of Mistakes. But after your work is done and you realize your blunders, don't shirk, don't whine, don't despond, but—

Study your Mistakes.

Then profit from them—and go ahead!

❖❖❖❖

Where will you be and what will you be doing ten years from today if you keep on doing what you are doing now?

—Napoleon Hill, 1883-1970

The person with a Definite Major Purpose, faith and determination may, because of circumstances beyond his control, be swept occasionally from the success side of this great river to the failure side, but he will not long remain there, for his mental reactions to his defeat will be sufficiently strong to carry him back to the success side where he rightfully belongs.

Realize that failure or defeat are only temporary—Nature's way of bringing out humility and wisdom and understanding. Realize too, that with every adversity there is the seed of an equivalent or greater benefit.

—Napoleon Hill, 1883-1970

❖❖❖❖

RUTS

One of the important lessons of this life is to learn to keep out of Ruts. Everyone is bound to strike them at times. But they should be gotten out of—immediately. For to stay in a Rut is to stick still—and stagnate, while others pass you and forget you.

Keep your eyes Open and your Mind Awake.

Watch out for the Imitation Rut—the Rut that takes you away from your own Work and your own Ideas and makes a Duplicate out of you instead of an Original. Creators stand in a class by themselves. Pay tribute to the Head on your own shoulders. Get the habit of Initiation.

Keep your Eyes Open and your Mind Awake.

Think. Get together new Ideas. Welcome them. Read. Profit from the Minds of past ages. Compare them with the advancing Thought and Experiences of your own age. Delve into the Mysteries. Seek out the Truths they hold. Learn SOMETHING new each day—and you will be ready—armed against getting into Ruts.

Keep your Eyes Open and your Mind Awake.

Vary your Work each day as greatly as possible. Think out new ways of doing old Tasks. The Brain acts spryest when it is most interested. Love your Work. If you don't, find Work that you do.

Keep your Eyes Open and your Mind Awake.

And be kind to your own human Machine. Give it Rest. Occasionally slip away into new Surroundings, see new Faces, and meet new Scenes. Find delight among those who Do and Dare. Lock arms with the Smilers—pass by the Frowners. Now, read this little talk over again—resolving that you will from this time on stay out of the Rut business.

❖❖❖❖

Never mistake motion for action.

—Ernest Hemingway, 1899-1961

Teamwork produces power, but whether the power is temporary or permanent depends upon the motive that inspired the cooperation. If the motive is one that inspires people to cooperate willingly, the power produced by this sort of Teamwork will endure as long as that spirit of willingness prevails. If the motive is one that forces people to cooperate, by fear or any other negative cause, the power produced will be temporary. Great physical power can be produced by coordination of the efforts of individuals, but the endurance of that power, its quality, scope, and strength, are derived from that intangible something known as the "spirit" in which people work together for the attainment of a common end. Where the spirit of Teamwork is willing, voluntary and free, it leads to the attainment of a power that is very great and enduring.

—Napoleon Hill, 1883-1970

❖❖❖❖

TOGETHER

For the sake of this little Talk, let us suppose that the one word *Together* is derived from the three words—TO GET THERE. It is quite possible, anyway. For when people get themselves Together, or you collect all your individual forces Together, the thing aimed at usually happens.

TO GET THERE is to get Together.

Analyze a Human Failure. Here is what you learn. He is all apart—all unhitched. His Brain is without organization. Most of his fine sensibilities are stunned or dead. His Will isn't Landlord any more. It's just a Boarder—and half starved at that. His original force of Executives and assistants—once alert and healthy and willing—have all gone out into the yard to Doze. Confusion and Ruin is everywhere. Chaos reigns. What is the Remedy? This—

TO GET THERE is to get Together.

It's marvelous the change that comes about when a man gets Together all his Forces and centers them upon the doing of ONE thing at a time. The Together idea is the progressive idea. "Where there is a Will, there is a Way." But the Will is of no use without the Plan back of the Will. Plan, Will—Way. All Together and things are accomplished.

TO GET THERE is to get Together.

When you begin to Divide your interests or to Distribute your forces, you begin to lose your Grip. As you draw all your Forces Together, you increase your Power. Big things are done on the Together plan. Bird shot will kill small game but it takes the single Rifle balls to bring down the big game.

TO GET THERE is to get Together.

Weigh and consider this thought as you face your work each day. Give it an honor place as a working rule. Get Together. Then stick Together.

21

❖❖❖❖

Where there is nothing to lose by trying, and a great deal to gain if successful, by all means try!

—Napoleon Hill, 1883-1970

Every person who wins in any undertaking must be willing to burn his ships and cut all sources of retreat. Only by so doing can one be sure of maintaining that state of mind known as a burning desire to win—essential to success.

—Napoleon Hill, 1883-1970

It is very important to expect to win or to accomplish each goal you set out to reach. Wanting to overcome obstacles will be more likely if you expect to win. One big reason for a winning attitude is that you will take the necessary steps and not quit when the going gets difficult.

—Don M. Green, Executive Director
Napoleon Hill Foundation

❖❖❖❖

WIN

The very first commandment in the decalogue of Winning is to—

Keep your Chin up!

Get busy at the first job that you run into or that runs into you. Tackle it "on all fours," if necessary. Center your whole enthusiasm in it. Study its every detail. Drive your very Heart interest into it. But don't forget to—

Keep your Chin up.

People who look down never get much of an idea of the sky where the Stars are set. And the fellow who doesn't hitch at least one or two of his wagons to a Star never gets very high up. Get your eyes off the ground. Look Ahead.

Keep your Chin up.

For, after all, Winning is a thing within—then out. No other man will or can Win for you. No other man in all the world, no matter how exalted, has the ability and power that is concentrated in you, waiting for some match of Action to touch it off. Also, your Success can be as the Success of no other man. But you alone must find the Thing and DO the Work. It's great fun, too, if you—

Keep your Chin up.

It is easier to Win than to Fail. Everybody sides with the Winner. But the Failure walks alone.

Keep your Chin up.

Remembering that to Win is to do your work well—today. The thing delayed or put off is the thing undone. Start right now. Straighten your shoulders. Set your eyes ahead. Clench your fist—close your jaw, and—

Keep your Chin up.

And you will WIN!

❖❖❖❖

The reason I beat the Austrians is, they didn't know the value, of five minutes.

—Napoleon Bonaparte, 1769-1821

As if you could kill time without injuring eternity.

—Henry David Thoreau, 1817-1862

Dost thou love life? Then do not squander time, for that's the stuff life is made of.

—Benjamin Franklin, 1706-1790

Success does not require a great amount of knowledge about anything, but it does call for the persistent use of whatever knowledge one may have. Successful people know themselves; not as they think they are, but as their habits have made them. Therefore, you should take inventory of yourself so that you may discover where and how you are using your time. These are questions which are important and claim earnest attention.

- *How are you using your time?*
- *How much of it are you wasting, and how are you wasting it?*
- *How are you going to stop this waste?*

—Napoleon Hill, 1883-1970

❖❖❖❖

Learn to use your Time.

For if you don't it passes on, never to return—coldly mindless of your sorrow and your regret. As steadily, silently and smoothly as does this aged Earth move in its path, so does Time move on. It never stops to tie its shoestrings. It never waits.

Time is Effort, harnessed and worked to a full day's portion.

Time has no Business, boasts no monied Millions, hires no fast-legged Errand Boys, houses no Clerks, thinks no Problems, rules no States. Time IS Business, Money, the Errand Boy, the Clerk, the Problem, the State!

Time is but the man in the job put to action and to work.

And Time used to profit Today will accumulate Power for you Tomorrow just as sure as Time goes on. Meditate not on Trifles. Attempt big things. Remembering that—

This day will never dawn again!

And yet, mighty as Time is, priceless in comparison to all else in the world, Time is the freest thing in existence. Perhaps that is why so many fail to grasp it with earnestness and with enthusiasm? Perhaps that is why so few realize its presence and let it pass on?

Think! No matter what your work today, if it is worth while at all—Time to plan it out, Time to do it well, and Time to finish it, is your day's greatest gift and your greatest job.

Learn to use your Time.

❖❖❖❖

There is only one success—to be able to spend your life in your own way.

—Christopher Morley, 1890-1957

Success is simply a matter of luck. Ask any failure.

—Earl Wilson, 1934-2005

Always bear in mind that your own resolution to success is more important than any other one thing.

—Abraham Lincoln, 1809-1865

Success is achieved and maintained by those who keep trying.

—Napoleon Hill, 1883-1970

Many people believe that material success is the result of favorable 'breaks' . . . The only 'break' anyone can afford to rely upon is a self-made 'break.' These come through the application of persistence. The starting point is definiteness of purpose.

—Napoleon Hill, 1883-1970

❖❖❖❖

SUCCESS

In Success, defeat is but an incident. Obstacles, stumbling blocks, disappointment in ideals—these things weave into and form the Raiment to Success. For Success is a series of failures—put to flight.

Learn to Walk past Failure.

A few years ago a young man stood behind a New England counter as a Clerk. Quiet, honest, faithful, yet a Failure in the eyes of his Employer, who one day drew aside the father of the boy and advised that the son be taken back to the farm for he never would become a Merchant. Today if you will but walk down State Street, Chicago, you will behold this young man's monument—a tribute to the failures, disappointments and iron persistence of Marshall Field, who died the greatest Merchant in the World.

Learn to Walk past Failure.

But Success isn't measured in tangible assets. Lincoln left next to nothing in money standards. His Success, though, is the marvel and inspiration of the Ages.

Learn to Walk past Failure.

Success is largely a matter of personal Viewpoint. It is impossible for you to fail permanently if you determine to Succeed. Let each new day of your life then, take invoice of its own self. Let it chalk up the Failures with the Successes—let it mark plainly the Record. But inside of your own consciousness let nothing take from the image of your mind, the Knowledge that real Success consists wholly in sacrificing temporarily in repeated failures that you may win permanently in worth while Deeds done.

Learn to Walk past Failure.

❖❖❖❖

A ship in harbor is safe—but that is not what ships are for.

—John A. Shedd, 1859-1928

The three enemies which you shall have to clear out—indecision, doubt and fear.

Fears are nothing more than states of mind, one's state of mind is subject to control and direction.

Man can create nothing which he does not first conceive in the form of an impulse or thought.

Nature has endowed man with absolute control over but one thing, and that is thought.

—Napoleon Hill, 1883-1970

Immortality is but a simple matter of Decision—a Decision to Dare.

Initiate—Dare.

All the world loves the man who isn't afraid to Dare—a man willing to start something without first waiting a week to figure out the cost. It always takes Courage—sometimes courage mixed with "blood and iron." But the man ready to Dare is the creator of great Events.

Initiate—Dare.

Better make mistakes—better blunder along making some healthy headway, than to fear Failure or grow timid and vacillating and flabby in the legs. Become a man of Daring and Doing and the Powers that are so latent in every human will rise to aid you and push you on.

Initiate—Dare.

You will never be Anything, unless you Dare Something.

Initiate—Dare.

Dare to attempt new things. Dare to try out new Jobs. Dare to go ahead, kicking aside Precedent if necessary, and you will have no time to shovel out of your path wrecked Hopes and dead Dreams. Dare to be a better man at your present task than the man who went before you. Dare to be a bigger man than the man above you. Be. But, if you are, you will first have to—

Initiate—Dare.

❖❖❖❖

Our doubts are traitors, and make us lose the good we oft might win by fearing to attempt.

—William Shakespeare, 1564-1616

Doubters are not builders! Had Columbus lacked self-confidence and faith in his own judgment, the richest and most glorious spot of ground on this earth might never have been discovered, and these lines might never have been written. Had George Washington and his compatriots of the 1776 historical fame not possessed Self-Confidence, Cornwallis's armies would have conquered and the United States of America would be ruled today from a little island lying three thousand miles away in the East.

—Napoleon Hill, 1883-1970

❖❖❖❖

BACKBONE

There are two kinds of Backbones—the one with the Back and no Bone and the one with Both Back and Bone! Backbone! what great things have been put across in your name!

Stiffen your Backbone.

It is a great thing to have a big Brain, a fertile Imagination, grand Ideals, but the man with these, bereft of a good Backbone is sure to serve no useful end.

Stiffen your Backbone.

There is a little vine that starts at the base of great trees. Then it climbs and twines about until it squeezes and saps away unto death the tree around which it clings. It has not a Backbone—no vital individual strength of its own, so it seeks out to tear down and kill where there is strength, power and life. That is what Backbone-less people do.

Stiffen your Backbone.

Use it to stand alone with. Use it to bolster up your own individual resources. Use it to strengthen weaker Backbones than your own. Use it for the working out of your entire Character. Then Deeds Done, will gather about you in Battalions, and Opportunity will stand around anxious to introduce you to her friends.

Stiffen your Backbone.

Use your Backbone at your job today—you who clerk, you whose fingers pound the type keys, you whose brains formulate plans, distribute details and master problems. For the temple of Success is upheld by the strong arms of men and women who have Backbone and use it.

❖❖❖❖

The truth is: A man is paid, not merely for that which he knows, but more particularly for what he does with what he knows, or that which he can get others to do.

—Napoleon Hill, 1883-1970

I have observed that men with college training who follow the habit of doing more than they are paid for, combining their college training with the advantages they gain from this habit, get ahead much more rapidly than men who do more than they are paid for but have no college training. From this I have reached the conclusion that there is a certain amount of thought discipline that a man gets from college training which men without this training do not generally possess.

—Napoleon Hill, 1883-1970

The subject of pay is easy to put in the right perspective if you would take time to read Ralph Waldo Emerson's Theory of Compensation.

—Don M. Green, Executive Director
Napoleon Hill Foundation

❖❖❖❖

Emerson says that "the strongest man on earth is the man who stands most alone." Owe money—be in Debt—and you stand by the props that the sweat of other men's brows and the gray of other men's brains have earned and bought. You don't stand alone. You play false to your own strength.

Abhor Debt. Pay.

Debt means to owe—somebody else. It means that you give up what might be yours. It means that you offer a part of yourself for sale for a definite sum. When you owe money you make yourself a slave. The other fellow holds you fast in literal bondage.

Abhor debt. Pay.

Better live happy away from glamour, smooth words, hand-clapping, and selfish gratification than Dog to some Master whose whistle you are bound to respect.

Abhor debt. Pay.

The quickest way to kill a Friend (the most valuable possession on Earth) is to ask him to lend you money. If he is a real Friend he will refuse. If you are a real Man you will learn a lesson and thank him. The man who makes it a rule to live within his means soon creates means to live out of it. There is but one safe, sound, sensible rule in money affairs and that is to pay as you go—or don't go!

Abhor debt. Pay.

Start today to Pay up. Will yourself to do it. Catch fire and enthusiasm from the freedom and power that follow in the way of the man who owes not a dollar to any man.

Abhor debt. Pay.

❖❖❖

There is very little difference in people, but that little difference makes a big difference. The little difference is attitude. The big difference is whether it is positive or negative.

—Napoleon Hill, 1883-1970

In examining our actions, we must avoid moaning about missed opportunities and roads not taken. Instead, take the positive approach suggested by the late newspaper columnist Arthur Brisbane, who wrote: "Regret for time wasted can become a power for good in the time that remains. And the time that remains is time enough if we will only stop the waste and the idle, useless regretting."

The secret of being able to correct our habits and begin making use of the time we would otherwise have wasted is to stay young in heart and in mind, no matter how long we have been around.

—W. Clement Stone, 1902-2002

When someone said that we make our habits, then our habits make us, they made a very true statement—whether it be a good habit like reading good books on a daily basis or a regular exercise, or a bad habit like using tobacco. These habits can have a tremendous effect on our lives—whether it be negative or positive—which is a choice we each make.

—Don M. Green, Executive Director
Napoleon Hill Foundation

❖❖❖

COUNT

If there IS any pure Luck in the world or if it ever really does figure in the summing up of things, here's when it figures biggest—on the day that you find your Life Work—and glory in it. Lucky you are, then—for you—Count. The world must have you.

Be Somebody in the Crowd—Count.

No man ever Counts until he assumes Responsibility. Responsibility demands the work of the Brain and Heart. These two, working together, breed Ideas. Then Results begin to show. And Results make you Count.

Be Somebody in the Crowd—Count.

People who are Useful always Count. So if you want to Count—if you want to be singled out and justly praised, think of the most useful service possible for you to render. Then get busy in doing it. You at your job, doing it as best you can, are sure to count.

Be Somebody in the Crowd—Count.

Nothing stirs and inspires more than to have it said that you are Somebody and that—you Count—that you are a Creator, a Builder, a Producer. Anyone is justified in congratulating himself if he does things—if he really Counts.

Be Somebody in the Crowd—Count.

But don't be so foolish as to be completely satisfied with the results of any work. Growth comes in a large measure by Comparison. When you do your work better Today than Yesterday you realize your genuine Capacity and know that there is no actual Perfection except the Perfection of doing better Today than Yesterday. Strive for this and you need have no concern as to whether or not you will Count. You will.

❖❖❖❖

*Ask yourself this question, "Am I a success or a failure?"
If you are a failure, no amount of explanation will change the
results, for the one thing the world will never forgive is failure.
The world wants successes; it worships successes, but it has no
time for failures. The only way one may explain away his
failure is by trimming his sails, through Self-Discipline, so the
circumstances of his life will lead him to success.*

*It is a great day in a person's life when he sits down
quietly and has a heart to heart talk with himself, for he is sure
to make discoveries about himself which will be helpful,
although his discoveries may give him a shake. Nothing is
ever accomplished by merely wishing, hoping, or day
dreaming. Earnest self-analysis helps one to rise above these.
No one can get something for nothing, although many have
tried to do so. Everything worth having has a definite price,
and that price must be paid. The circumstances of one's life
make this essential.*

—Napoleon Hill, 1883-1970

*What we desire in life is obtainable if we are willing to pay
the price. Whether it be weight control, financial security or
some other milepost we wish to reach. It will only be
accomplished provided we pay the price. Discipline in our
lives is a necessity to reach goals that are worthy of our time
and efforts. But do not expect to get what you want without
paying the price. This is a very simple but important lesson.*

—Don M. Green, Executive Director
Napoleon Hill Foundation

❖❖❖❖

WHY

Before you do a thing—ask Why?

A great deal of the Lost Motion of the world results from Head-long Action—going into a task without Cause—without some definite Purpose—without first finding out—Why.

Before you do a thing—ask Why?

Let Why lead you on and save you Power. Simply answer with promptness its Silent questionings. Give unto Why a substantial reason for the fiber that is within you.

Before you do a thing—ask Why?

Ask yourself: "Why should I do this thing? Why should I refuse to do it?" Put your actions to the Why test. Think of the wealth of happiness that the habitual use of Why can bring you!

Before you do a thing—ask Why?

Make Why very personal. "Why do I squander so much Time? Why do I appreciate so little the chance to Live? Why do I use so small a fraction of my Brain Ability? Why do I not make more Friends? Why do I worry about things that Never Happen? Why do I scold when I should Cheer?" Why?

Before you do a thing—ask Why?

Keep Why busy about your House. And at the Nightfall of each day gather into convention the Whys of each Thought and Act.

Before you do a thing—ask Why?

Eliminate the regretful Why. Put yourself on the Stand hourly. Ask and Answer with fortitude and freedom—unafraid of Right conscientiously performed.

❖❖❖❖

One key to effective public communication is maintaining an "open face," says Arch Lustberg, former Catholic University speech professor and now a consultant to the U.S. Chamber of Commerce.

In his book **Winning When It Really Counts**, *Lustberg points out there are three possible facial positions: the closed face, the neutral face and the open face.*

The face you present to an audience can have a significant impact on your message. Audiences instinctively assume that "you can learn a great deal of what's going on in a person's mind by the expression on his face."

The **closed face** *results from the creation of a vertical line between the brows, the frown line. You do this when you draw your eyes into narrow slits and tighten the brow muscles.*

You slip into a closed face when you think, when you feel worried, when you're angry. Lustberg says, "It's a terrible expression for an audience to see."

The **neutral face** *looks dead—nothing moves but the mouth. The look is common among television newscasters. The neutral face is cold and expressionless, nevertheless, it's the expression most people use in public speaking.*

With the **open face**, *your eyebrows are elevated and horizontal lines appear in your forehead. Lustberg points out that people open their faces a lot when they're in animated conversation, talking to a baby, playing with a kitten or puppy or telling a favorite story.*

—Napoleon Hill, 1883-1970

❖❖❖❖

The most marvelous of all pieces of work is the human Face. Strange that out of all the billions of Faces made since Time got to going, no two Faces have ever been exactly alike. Strange, too, that no one Face long remains the same!

The Face is the Revelation of Character. As surely and positively as does the hand guided by the orders of the Brain clear wide wastes, build great cities, and cut into life-like figures from bare rocks the story of men's achievements, so does the Brain and Thought of a man carve and fashion daily the secret workings of his Ideals and Purposes into the Lines and Planes of his own Face.

Make Something of YOUR Face.

The only way to make Something of your Face is to make Something of your Character.

A Face never lies. It may be a Comic Picture, a Comedy of Errors, a Shakespearean Tragedy, a chiseled piece of Power, or a wrecked god—but it is no lie. If you would know your Friend, study the history of his Face.

Make Something of YOUR Face.

No one could get a hearing if he wrote a whole library of malicious tales about Lincoln. His wonderful Face would contradict them all. To learn what manner of person a man is, study his Face. His Character is proclaimed there as Trumpet Tones. Pope said that the proper study of mankind was man. But the way to study a man is to study his Face. Be not so foolish as to try to "hop bail" on your own Face. You can't. Better start associating more with it. It is your largest asset, for no man can take it from you. Realize now, then, that the most important job for you each day is to—

Make SOMETHING of your Face.

❖❖❖❖

The heights by great men reached and kept were not attained by sudden flight. But they, while their companions slept, were toiling toward the night.

—Henry Wadsworth Longfellow, 1807-1882

Emerson said, "Do the thing and you shall have the power." He never expressed a more truthful thought than this. Moreover, it applies to every calling, and to every human relationship. Men who gain and hold power do so by making themselves useful to others. All this talk about men holding fat jobs through, "pull," is nonsense. A man may procure a good job through pull, but take my word for it when I tell you that if he remains in the job he will do so through "push," and the more of it he puts into the job, the higher he will rise.

—Napoleon Hill, 1883-1970

❖❖❖❖

RESPONSIBILITY

A great man by the name of Ansalus de Insulis—remember the name—once wrote these wonderful words: "Learn as if you were to live forever; live as if you were to die tomorrow."

Be Responsible, first, to Yourself.

Responsibility is one thing that all must face and that none can escape. It starts with the baby in the cradle. It never ends! For the Responsibility of a man goes on even after his work in the flesh is over. A man performs a great deed. It lives in printed pages and goes on in its influence as long as there is any life in the world at all.

Be Responsible, first, to Yourself.

Individual Responsibility! It's the thing that makes the Man. Without it there is no Man. Bear in mind, you who must realize Responsibility to your Employer, or to your Friend, or to your Home,—your first Responsibility is to Yourself. And if you are weak and false to yourself—if you wabble in doing the things that mean your very life and Success—you are already a Failure.

Be Responsible, first, to Yourself.

Then FEEL your Responsibility. No one is useless who believes that some things depend upon him alone. You who read this little preachment, take it to heart. Be unafraid of at least attempting larger things. Convince your own self that you have worth and can prove it—and the tasks of big moment will take care of you and lift you into importance and affluence—the gifts of having the courage to take Responsibility and shoulder it. But, remember to—

Be Responsible, first, to Yourself.

❖❖❖❖

The only true happiness comes from squandering ourselves for a purpose.

—William Cowper, 1731-1800

*A man's happiness and peace of mind depend on his sharing all kinds of wealth. Business relations cannot properly be described as a relationship of **love** between buyer and seller; yet when the idea of **service to one's fellow men** comes into the relationship, much that is profitable to both parties also enters in. "A little bit of myself," said Henry Ford, "goes into every automobile that rolls off our assembly lines, and I think of every automobile we sell, not in terms of the profit it yields us, but in terms of the useful service it may render the purchaser." Thomas A. Edison said: "I never perfected an invention that I did not think about in terms of the service it might give others."*

— Napoleon Hill, 1883-1970

❖❖❖❖

HAPPINESS

Happiness is Helpfulness bubbling over at the rim. Also, Happiness is getting in tune with the music of the Band of The-Out-of-Doors. There is no unhappiness in Nature.

Lend a Hand. Make Happiness a Habit.

The people who are Happy are the people who are Successful—not in money, merely, but in Contentment, realized Aims and completed Effort. To win—be Happy. To be Happy—do something worth while.

Lend a Hand. Make Happiness a Habit.

The fastest growing concern is the one with the most Happy helpers. Happiness produces health. Health plows up the field of native ability and makes ready the soil for the Happy Harvest.

Lend a Hand. Make Happiness a Habit.

Happiness cannot be bought. Being rated as of all things about the most Precious—it is at the same time free. It is for all. But there must be mustered the effort to take it. And after you have it, if you would keep it—give it away.

Lend a Hand. Make Happiness a Habit.

For Happiness boiled down is nothing more nor less than being well content with your progress by seeking better things all the time, being glad that you are alive, thanking God that you have a chance, believing that you have some things that nobody else in all the world has, and just resolving that you are going to make this world a marvelous place to stay in for a while. It's also having something that everyone else will want—and giving it to others.

Lend a Hand. Make Happiness a Habit.

❖❖❖❖

Drive thy business or it will drive thee.

—Benjamin Franklin, 1706-1790

By rendering more service and better service than that for which you are paid, you thereby take advantage of the Law of Increasing Returns through the operation of which you will eventually be paid, in one way or another, for far more service than you actually perform.

—Napoleon Hill, 1883-1970

Giving better service than others will put you ahead in your field. The results may not show themselves after one day, one week, or one month but giving better service over a period of time will provide dividends. The job you are doing does not matter—whether you are a waiter or a banker—your efforts will not go unrewarded for long. The Law of Compensation is as natural and works as dependable as the Law of Gravity.

—Don M. Green, Executive Director
Napoleon Hill Foundation

❖❖❖❖

SERVICE

To serve is to find Something to do—and then do it. It matters not what this Something is, so long as it serves a Useful end.

Honor your Job.

The biggest man or woman who ever lived, was in no way, after all, greater than a Servant—in some way or other. The world is a world of Servants. You are a Servant. The one you Serve is a Servant.

Honor your Job.

Proportionately every man is as great as the greatest if he Serves to his fullest Capacity. To do this is to Grow. And Growth only comes to the people of Capacity. You who do your best today will do better tomorrow. To Service there is no limit.

Honor your Job.

No occupation is so dignified as Service of some kind. Nothing brings greater rewards in Happiness and Power. He climbs highest who helps another up.

Honor your Job.

The truest fact in all this world is that the more you do for someone else, the more you boost your own game—the stronger your own individual influence and Character becomes. Suppose you try it out today and learn for yourself. Try it in your Home, at your Office, in your place of power or in the midst of the humblest circumstances. Be a real Servant. Serve. And be glad in doing it.

Honor your Job.

And by so doing become one of the factors in the stirring affairs of your time.

❖❖❖❖

Ideas are the only assets which have no fixed values. All achievements begin as ideas. The Science of Success Course is designed to induce a flow of ideas through your mind. It is intended to introduce you to your other self, the self who has a vision of your innate spiritual powers. The self who will not accept or recognize failure, but will arouse your determination to go forth and claim that which is rightfully yours.

Ideas form the foundation of all fortunes and the starting point of all inventions. They have mastered the air above us and the waters of the ocean around us. There can be no evolution of any idea without a starting point in the form of Definiteness of Purpose. Therefore, this principle takes first position in the Philosophy of Personal Achievement.

—Napoleon Hill, 1883-1970

The author Orison Swett Marden wrote that we must have castles in the air before we can have castles on the ground. Napoleon Hill wrote thoughts are things. He said the same thing as Marden, which is everything begins in our thought process.

—Don M. Green, Executive Director
Napoleon Hill Foundation

❖❖❖❖

46

IMAGINATION

Imagination is the greatest asset that the world's Doers have ever had. Money, titles, estates—they are all cheap beside this marvelous gift. Imagination is the creator of them all in most instances.

Cultivate your Imagination.

People do the things they first see done with their Imagination. McAdoo with the eye of his mind saw rapid cars taking thousands of people daily under the Hudson river. Of course, people turned their heads and smiled at his dream. But McAdoo made real his dream in the Hudson tunnels. Marconi saw the messages of people thousands of miles away floating on the waves of the air and sounded off at a marvelous instrument. He was at once rated as crazy. But he went ahead and presented to an astonished world the unbelievable Wireless telegraph!

People call America the "land of Opportunity." It is the land of Imagination. Here the humblest rises to the greatest position of power. It's the working of Imagination that contributes most. The obscure clerk sees himself President of the concern he serves. Then he advances step by step until he realizes his aim. His first step toward the President's job was to see himself with his Imagination, occupying it.

Cultivate your Imagination.

The great Perthes once said "that a quick Imagination is the salt of earthly life, without which nature is but a skeleton; but the higher the gift the greater the responsibility."

Cultivate it in little things. Then the little things will become big things. Then the big things will take their place among the undying things. History is but the story of the achievements of people who had Imagination.

Cultivate your Imagination.

❖❖❖❖

Men may doubt what you say, but they will believe what you do.

— Lewis Cass, 1782–1866

Determine that the thing can and shall be done, and then we shall find the way.

— Abraham Lincoln, 1809-1865

Nature has endowed man with absolute control over but one thing, and that is thought. This fact, coupled with the additional fact that everything which man creates begins in the form of a thought, leads one very near to the principle by which fear may be mastered.

If it is true that all thought has a tendency to clothe itself in its physical equivalent (and this is true, beyond any reasonable room for doubt), it is equally true that thought impulses of fear and poverty cannot be translated into terms of courage and financial gain.

— Napoleon Hill, 1883-1970

❖❖❖❖

GHOSTS

There is nothing in Ghosts. But they do exist. Ghosts are nothing more nor less than the phantom Imaginations of sick, afraid Minds. They go by various names—Failure Ghosts, Idea Ghosts, Mistake Ghosts, Chance Ghosts, Regret Ghosts—and Millions of others.

Face your Ghosts.

Walk right up to your Ghosts. Shake hands with them. Look them in the eye. Give them a hearing. And then kick them out—for they never will do you any good.

Face your Ghosts.

Ghosts are always on the Job. In the office of the Doctor, Lawyer, Business man, in your Home, on the Street—everywhere. But Ghosts get uneasy in the Light. They are born and bred in the Dark Alleys and exist only by the Sandbag. Your cue is to keep the Lights turned on—your Mind open—your Courage alert—your Character Impregnable.

Face your Ghosts.

Today when you read your newspapers there will be Ghosts between the Lines of the Print. Ghosts seek you out and constantly try for your scalp. They like Time-Wasters, the Man-Afraid-of-His-Job Hesitaters. They revel among the players of idle Good-fellowship. But Ghosts sneak like cowed dogs with their tails between their legs, at the sight of Doers, Time Users, Obstacle Riddlers, and Path Makers. Be unafraid of Ghosts.

Face your Ghosts.

But don't harbor them. Live, Red-Blooded Men can't be dragging around a lot of Ghosts and amount to Anything.

Face your Ghosts.

❖❖❖❖

*When I approach a child, he inspires in me two
sentiments: tenderness for what he is, and respect for what he
may become.*

—Louis Pasteur, 1822-1895

*It is inevitable that people who dislike others will be
disliked. Through the principle of telepathy, every mind
communicates with all other minds within its range. The
person who wishes to develop an attractive personality is
under the constant necessity of controlling not only his words
and deeds, but, of course, his thoughts as well.*

—Napoleon Hill, 1883-1970

❖❖❖❖

RESPECT

Respect is the name of the Fellow who tends door for your Conscience. His is the most sacred Office in the gift of your Character. For, when he goes wrong, Conscience becomes ill unto Death.

Nothing of Winning matters with Respect gone.

Respect is your most faithful Friend, your greatest Guide, your most powerful Protector—your safest Pilot into Port.

Nothing of Winning matters with Respect gone.

And Respect is made at home. You are your own Respect. For a man can be on no better terms with anybody than with his Own Self. The Man without Respect is a Make-believe, a Fraud—a Counterfeit.

Nothing of Winning matters with Respect gone.

Respect yourself and other people will be compelled to Respect you—and you will Respect them. Respect is the beginning of Wisdom. With Respect on guard, you look people squarely in the Eye without wavering. With Respect, active and unafraid, you go ahead to move away Rubbish and Obstacles and pave a Path for other people to walk in from which they profit.

Nothing of Winning matters with Respect gone.

Think about this as you move about Today. Let it keep you Strong. Let it make you indomitable. Let it lift you from your present position into one higher up. Let it make of you a Leader. For—

Nothing of Winning matters with Respect gone.

❖❖❖❖

Leadership is a potent combination of strategy and character, but if you must be without one, be without the strategy.

—Gen. H. Norman Schwarzkoff

This is one trait of personality for which satisfactory substitute has never been found because it is something that reaches deeper into a human being than most qualities of personality. Yes, Sincerity begins with oneself and is a trait of sound character that reflects itself so visibly that none can fail to observe it. Be Sincere first of all with yourself; be Sincere with those to whom you are related by family ties; be Sincere with your daily associates in connection with your occupation; be Sincere with your friends and acquaintances; and, of course, with your country. Above all, be Sincere with the Giver of all gifts to mankind.

—Napoleon Hill, 1883-1970

❖❖❖❖

LINCOLNIZE

A man is always bigger than anything big that he does. No man will ever be able to create anything greater than his own Character. To take a single illustration— Lincoln. To Humanity, Abraham Lincoln is infinitely finer than President Lincoln, and as the years accumulate, deeper and deeper do his superb qualities penetrate into the innermost workings of the peoples and nations of the world.

Lincolnize your Work.

The rules of action that guided Lincoln were the rules of ordinary Sense and Humanity. They were unvarnished. They were disguised by no extra trappings and encumbrances. The simplest thinking person immediately grasped the just rulings and conclusions of Lincoln. The best investment that any Business House can make is to gather together the simple rules of conduct that guided Lincoln, and have them Printed, Framed and Hung, before the faces of every one of its Employees.

Lincolnize your Business.

When Lincoln promoted General Hooker he told him that he was doing it in spite of the fact that he had glaring Faults, Enemies, Vanities, and a lot of other things. Lincoln recognized the high qualities of Leadership that Hooker had and he was not blinded by his defects. He always saw the Big things in a man. He knew Grant even before he had met him. He felt men by their Deeds. Results to him reflected the man.

Lincolnize your Judgment.

Lincoln was Just. Lincoln was Generous. Lincoln was Square. Lincoln was Magnanimous. Lincoln was Modest. Lincoln was Gentle. Lincoln was Strong.

Lincolnize your Ideas.

❖❖❖❖

One of the greatest leaders who ever lived stated the secret of his leadership in six words, as follows: "Kindness is more powerful than compulsion."

—Napoleon Hill, 1883-1970

A Pleasing Personality is not window dressing. It can only be created through embracing attitudes and habits everyone needs. You will not lose yourself in the new personality you forge; rather, you will define yourself—your successful self—in terms of exactly what and who you wish to be.

—Napoleon Hill, 1883-1970

❖❖❖❖

SINCERITY

Be Sincere.

For it's the mark that stamps and "Trademarks" your Character so that it stands at once as Genuine.

Be Sincere.

Nobody trusts the man who doesn't trust himself. Be Sincere. Look the other fellow in the eye squarely and with confidence, and he will trust you.

Be Sincere.

Lacks in ability and knowledge are many times excused. But insincerity—never. Be Sincere. Teach the world once for all that you are square—Sincere—and the "order of business" for you will move smoothly and with satisfaction.

Be Sincere.

Sincerity is more than money. Even as the magnet attracts and clusters to itself particles of steel, so does the man who holds Sincerity as his asset, draw Men and Chances and great Works to his record.

Be Sincere.

Trouble yourself not that Yesterday was a failure. Today faces you. Try a new instrument. Tighten new cords for a new Tune. Take hold on a new Force—be Sincere. Then will this day have been far from in vain.

Be Sincere.

❖❖❖❖

Never give in. Never. Never. Never. Never.

—Winston Churchill, 1874-1965

As you charge your mind with ideas of success, the prospect of failure is unpleasant. But everyone experiences defeats, some large, some small. What separates those who ultimately achieve their dreams from those who stumble and leave the race is the ability to learn important lessons from what Shakespeare called "the slings and arrows of outrageous fortune."

Though it may seem ironic for a philosophy of success to extol the significance of failure, it should be considered an essential experience, one that could be built upon for the ultimate achievement of great things. What matters most when you suffer defeats is not the extent of your losses, but your ability to examine them and learn from what they teach you.

—Napoleon Hill, 1883-1970

If you are working to achieve a worthy goal and are ready to give up, take a few minutes to reflect. Read the story of Thomas Edison and the light bulb. Read Helen Keller's life story and you should be inspired to continue on your journey.

—Don M. Green, Executive Director
Napoleon Hill Foundation

❖❖❖❖

DIG

Dig.

Dig right through every obstacle. Fight to uphold the dignity of your Purpose. Dig, bore, squeeze, sweat—but get through!

Dig.

The regular, persistent drop of water will wear away the hardest stone. Science says that the even, rhythmic step of an army has power to start the wreck of the strongest bridge. In like manner does determined effort win anything—anywhere. To believe so, start today to—

Dig.

Dig! You see the other fellow carrying away plenty of "Bacon?" Dig. You failed in many things yesterday? Dig. You want money, reputation, glory? Dig. Mental, moral, or financial Bankruptcy stares boldly at you? Pay no attention. Just—

Dig.

Success is not a thing inherited. To get it you must—

Dig.

Dig.

Every man or woman who ever won at anything knew how to—Dig. It is the "A"-word of the Alphabet of Doing. Dig. No matter WHAT you want or WHERE you want it, or WHEN you want it, you must first know how to Dig—or you won't get it. Dig.

Dig.

❖❖❖❖

Concentration is the focusing of the attention, interest and desire upon the attainment of a definite end.

—Napoleon Hill, 1883-1970

Concentration is defined as "the habit of planting in the mind a definite aim, object or purpose, and visualizing the same until ways and means for its realization have been created."

The principle of concentration is the medium by which procrastination is overcome. The same principle is the foundation upon which both self-confidence and self-discipline are predicted.

The Law of Habit. The principle of habit and the principle of concentration go hand in glove. Habit may grow out of concentration and concentration may grow out of habit.

—Napoleon Hill, 1883-1970

❖❖❖❖

CONCENTRATE

Concentrate.

With steadiness, courage, dare-determinedness burn a hole into things. No matter what the thing at hand may be.

Concentrate.

The Wheel of Action and of Business moves by steady turns around one central hub. In Success, Rim, Spoke, Hub hold tight together, and as though human, Think, Plan, Move as one.

Concentrate.

Results come always to the persistent. Opportunity goes out of its way to get hold of the hand of the Sticker. The eye of the Boss is drawn irresistibly to the desk of the Doer. Concentrate.

Concentrate.

Draw the details together. Formulate your day's Plan. Strike a pace. Make every minute and every move count. Concentrate. And the finished Job will be the day's Goal—twenty-four hours of life well worth while.

Concentrate.

❖❖❖❖

I learned the way a monkey learns—by watching his parents.

—Queen Elizabeth II

Do you realize the power your subconscious mind contains—a power which you can tap and utilize? Do you recognize the source of power for achievement and success that can be gained by pooling your mind's resources with the resources of others for mutual benefit?

The power for all achievement, the power that you need in order to understand and apply the philosophy of success is readily available. The power you need for a productive life is in the storehouse of your own mind.

—Napoleon Hill, 1883-1970

Education is a way of life. It is easy to feel educated when one gets a degree, but the ceremony at which a degree is obtained is properly called a commencement exercise. This is simply a beginning, and education is a way of life.

—Don M. Green, Executive Director
Napoleon Hill Foundation

❖❖❖❖

LEARN

Be an Observer. Let nothing new appear without first clinching its value, studying its meaning, and absorbing its lesson. Learn.

Find Out.

Learn from Nature, People, Happenings. Read the thought of each day as far as you can fathom. Then apply your Knowledge. Learn all the time from everything you can—everywhere. Investigate the Mysteries, master the Difficulties.

Find Out.

Right now—a paragraph from History. John Milton—a word from you. "I am blind, past fifty, but I am completing my 'Paradise Lost'." Michael Angelo—your testimony. "Though seventy years of age, I am still learning." John Kemble—what have you to say? "Since leaving the stage, I have written out Hamlet thirty times. I am now beginning to understand my art!" You who have eyes, and ears, and mouths to talk with—Learn.

Find Out.

Your work today may look useless. You may be "only a Clerk." But you will always be one if you fail to Learn. For the Path of advancement marks the Way of the man Learn.

Find Out.

Leadership comes solely to those who KNOW Knowledge is surely Power. The Diners at the Table of the Feast of Success are no favored folk—none other than those who took the time to Learn. You—if you would Win—Learn!

❖❖❖❖

Man is what he believes.

—Anton Pavlovich Chekhov, 1860-1904

The ancestor of every action is a thought.

—Ralph Waldo Emerson, 1803-1882

*When Henley wrote the prophetic lines, "I am the master of my fate, I am the captain of my soul," he should have informed us that we are the masters of our fate, the captains of our souls, **because** we have the power to control our thoughts.*

*He should have told us that our brains become magnetized with the dominating thoughts which we hold in our minds, and, by means with which no man is familiar, these "magnets" attract to us the forces, the people, the circumstances of life which harmonize with the nature of our **dominating** thoughts.*

He should have told us that before we can accumulate riches in great abundance, we must magnetize our minds with intense desire for riches that we must become "money conscious" until the desire for money drives us to create definite plans for acquiring it.

—Napoleon Hill, 1883-1970

❖❖❖❖

People are paid, ambition is achieved, success comes only in the measure that a man Thinks.

Think.

All great Doers were and are great Thinkers. Think. Mistakes, Confusion, Consternation are rare callers at the brain of the man who Thinks.

Think.

But think to a definite purpose. Systematize your ideas. Plan out the acts of each of your minutes, and hours—and days. Think.

Think.

Napoleon was a Thinker. Sought out one day in one of the crises of France, he was found in an obscure garret, studying the streets of Paris and Thinking out his best moves for the morrow. Think.

Think.

Be your own Silent partner. Think. Be responsible to your own Intellectual Force. Think. Forge from the anvil of your own hard fights and failures, the Deeds of Doing that can only come after the most rigid and painstaking Thoughts. Think.

Think.

Start this day with the resolve to Think out each act you perform, knowing that the largest and most useful Results follow the man who Thinks.

❖❖❖❖

A wise man will make more opportunities than he finds.

—Sir Francis Bacon, 1561-1626

No great man ever complains of want of opportunity.

—Ralph Waldo Emerson, 1803-1882

If your ship doesn't come in, swim out to it!

—Jonathan Winters

Success sneaks in is one of the tricks of opportunity. It has a sly habit of slipping in by the back door, and often it comes disguised in the form of misfortune, or temporary defeat.

—Napoleon Hill, 1883-1970

Opportunities are so plentiful today that almost anyone can follow a career that would not have existed a few years ago. Many people have several different fields of work during their working lives and can change jobs readily and almost at will if they prepare through proper education and training.

—Don M. Green, Executive Director
Napoleon Hill Foundation

❖❖❖❖

OPPORTUNITY

Opportunity is a Something—not a nothing; also, something Real—not a Phantom.

And, too, Opportunity is an Ever-present—here today and here tomorrow. By moments, hours, days, weeks, months—years, she hovers about, unseen and unheard—except as her Spirit is felt and—seized!

Opportunity is the hand of Progress to the alert, and the "handwriting on the wall" of Failure, to the groggy and the slothful. For of all Messengers of Light she—Opportunity—is the one most patient, most fair, most just and most considerate.

Opportunity is no respecter of persons or of seasons. She is ever on the job and she ever waits and waits and waits. The man may fall forever asleep—but Opportunity—never.

At this actual minute she stands before YOU. All through the livelong day she will be at your call. Lightning-like she flashes her Messages to all—but her sole appeal is—to you.

Think! How about it? "Stop, look, listen"—can you see, hear, feel, grip her hand? Make the most of what she holds this day for you. Think—think, think! Then ACT.

For Opportunity, converted into a Fact, is the taking hold on the simplest task at hand—and doing it to a finish in the best way you know how. It's picking up the pins of Priceless Minutes that the other fellow passes heedlessly over. It's doing your work BETTER than you are paid for, and tackling bigger jobs than you may think you are capable of handling.

Great is the rise of the man who makes an early friend of Opportunity and takes her with him through the paths of the common everyday.

❖❖❖❖

Now here is a fine point most people tend to overlook. Until a man begins to render more service than that for which he is paid, he is already receiving full pay for that which he does. The sad fact is that 98 out of 100 wage earners have no Definite Purpose greater than that of working for a daily wage. Therefore, no matter how much work they do or how well they do it, the wheel of fortune turns past them without giving them more than a bare living because they neither expect nor demand more.

—Napoleon Hill, 1883-1970

The writer Elbert Hubbard admonished employees to be loyal to their employer or to do himself and his employer a favor by quitting and going elsewhere to work. Being loyal is important because if an employee is not in a good frame of mind he will not perform and grow. The pay one receives is not for the number of hours but the worth of his labor.

—Don M. Green, Executive Director
Napoleon Hill Foundation

❖❖❖❖

LOYALTY

Be Loyal.

To be Loyal is to be square with yourself. And you cannot be square with yourself without being a pretty good sort of a Boss—of yourself. The trouble with the people that fail is that they let someone else run their shop. Then dis-loyalty creeps in and sours and sucks and saps the life of a man away from himself.

Be Loyal.

You know your own possibilities better than any living being. Get next to them without delay and learn to be Loyal to them. It's a quality beyond price—this Loyalty.

Be Loyal.

The Loyal man oft times is of all men with discouragement tempted. But the fellow who sticks to his Faith and is Loyal—is the man that finally feels Growth and Equipment and Power becoming a part of himself.

Be Loyal.

Loyalty means sacrifice. But sacrifice means Success!

Be Loyal.

The steps of Achievement and Honor and Satisfaction are all rock riveted to Loyalty—Loyalty to your Work, and to your Friends.

Be Loyal.

Benefits redound to the fit and worthy. Your work today may seem mean and obscure indeed to yourself. But "the gods see everywhere" and the least neglect or slight to what you hold in hand today, may reflect and loom large in the completed work. Loyal attention from the start to the finish is the safest, fairest and surest path for you to pursue. Do but this and Results will take jealous care of you.

Be Loyal.

❖❖❖❖

Courage is rightly esteemed the first of human qualities because it is the quality which guarantees all others.

—Winston Churchill, 1874-1965

Considering that most of us often seem to be two people (or sometimes more) within our own minds, it is not unusual that many of us, at many times, are confused about who or what—and to what extent—WE ARE. To find one's real self is a priceless accomplishment. Never to find individuality is a tragic oversight. To become acquainted with the finest, strongest, most powerful being within us is a challenge, but an exciting and a rewarding one. If you can find and follow the instincts of your best self, all things can be yours. Your finest self can help to conquer fear, worry, indecision. It can lead you to a better understanding of the profound power of life, and can provide you with the mastery you need to be successful in whatever field you desire. Your best self is your most powerful ally.

—Napoleon Hill, 1883-1970

❖❖❖❖

COURAGE

Have Courage.

Courage is the art of sitting calmly in your seat without stirring and without getting excited when the Brass Band of Popularity, or Temporary Success or Ridicule goes by your house and turns around the corner. Courage steps out of the crowd. It stands alone.

Courage is native Nerve—refined.

Courage is neither bulldozing nor bare bluff—it's not related to either. Courage isn't physical merely, but moral—mostly.

Courage is naked Right put through fire and brought out uncracked and unbroken.

Courage is heartworth making itself felt in deeds. It never waits for chances; it makes chances.

A day without some Courage sprinkled in it is a day little worth while. For Courage makes the Man—and there never was a real Man that didn't have Courage.

Courage is a thing born in you—but it is also a thing much lustered by use and cultivation.

Today, tomorrow—and every day—have Courage. It makes the heart glad and the soul strong. It starts smiles in the system and stirs up the kind of circulation in a man that makes him go out and do his best at the most humble undertaking.

You can never fail if you have Courage—but you can never win without it.

Have Courage!

❖❖❖❖

To one who has faith, no explanation is necessary. To one without faith, no explanation is possible.

—Saint Thomas Aquinas, 1225-1274

*Here is a most significant fact—the subconscious mind takes any orders given it in a spirit of absolute faith and acts upon those orders, although the orders often have to be presented **over and over again,** through repetition, before they are interpreted by the subconscious mind.*

—Napoleon Hill, 1883-1970

Faith in yourself is a necessary giant leap if you expect to travel the success journey. Belief is a component that is an absolute need if maximum positive results are obtained. The statement, "I will believe it when I see it" should be, "I will see it when I believe it." A belief in what you are doing is of extreme importance.

—Don M. Green, Executive Director
Napoleon Hill Foundation

❖❖❖❖

Have Faith.

First, Faith in yourself, then Faith in the thing you set out to do—then Faith in the result.

Faith is the ability to believe you have won before you have. It's the art of beating the enemy, the obstacles, or the plan of your opposers, before they have securely organized. For Faith is to take victory in hand at the start.

Have Faith.

The great stories of Success from the beginning of time are but narratives of men and women doers—who had Faith. Faith feeds the hungry in adversity—clothes and warms the needy in temporary failure. For faith builds. It cannot destroy.

Have Faith.

Your success is limited only by your Faith. The results from Faith live limitless. Take heart.

Have Faith.

The only time people fail is when they lose Faith. The Pitcher in a ball game, the Soldier on a battle-field, the Leader in Politics, the Executive at the head of a task or business—the humblest Toiler—each goes ahead and does his best only as he is inspired to it by Faith. First, as he has it—then as those about, under or near him have Faith in him.

Have Faith.

And make it a vital part of your determination to Win, today. The most obscure worker is entitled to as great credit for results in proportion, as the man who commands—so long as he has and uses all the Faith he can muster. So, remember to keep a good stock of Faith on hand constantly. All this day long—

Have Faith.

❖❖❖❖

We act as though comfort and luxury were the chief requirements of life, when all we need to make us happy is something to be enthusiastic about.

—Charles Kingsley, 1819-1875

Are you enthusiastic about yourself? *Enthusiasm flows contagiously from one mind to another, and that is how we generally see it in action.* *Still—have you tried being enthusiastic about yourself?* *With something behind it?*

It can be a good deal of fun, and very instructive, to take that step back from **yourself,** *as though stepping out of your own skin, and then look at the person who bears your name.*

—Napoleon Hill, 1883-1970

Ralph Waldo Emerson said that nothing great was ever achieved without enthusiasm.

If you want to achieve anything worthwhile, choose something that you can be enthusiastic about, and you will be off to a great start.

Many people choose a path to please others or to make a great deal of money. *A better bet would be to choose a pursuit for which you have enthusiasm.*

—Don M. Green, Executive Director
Napoleon Hill Foundation

❖❖❖❖

ENTHUSIASM

Enthusiasm is what happens to a man when on taking invoice, he discovers that his Heart and Head and Determination have finally welded into and become a part of "the Main Chance."

Enthusiasm is a process—not merely a condition.

Most everybody has a Head and Heart and Determination—but it's the folks that have sufficient sense to get these together in the same spot at the same time for the same purpose that start things and move on the progress of the times.

Enthusiasm is the spark that starts the Action that moves the Man that finds the Cows and brings them home. Enthusiasm is what makes a fellow "get there."

Get Enthusiasm and you will "steam on." Nobody can stop you.

Enthusiasm is what goes through stone walls, bores miles under great rivers, wins battles and lays out cities and towns and nations. Enthusiasm changes maps and makes History possible.

You at your desk, at your plow, at your broom, at your axe, at your bat, at your pen—you, no matter who or where you are—take heart and hope and—Enthusiasm.

For Enthusiasm starts things, shapes things—does things.

Start today to mix Enthusiasm in your blood.

Then keep it there!

❖❖❖❖

The first blow is half the battle.

—Oliver Goldsmith, 1728-1774

We will either find a way, or make one.

—Hannibal, 247-183 B.C.

Whenever you meet a misfortune, put it into your past. Keep your mind upon future achievement, and you will find that mistakes of the past often work to fill the future with good fortune. Your wealth and your peace of mind are strongly connected with each other. Even at the lowest-level jobs, your success waits within your own mind. Add value to your work and you set in motion the forces that make the concepts of your mind turn into the realities of living.

—Napoleon Hill, 1883-1970

❖❖❖❖

I WILL

I will—make this day Worth While.

I will drop the Past, remembering it only as a valuable path through which I have walked into the Now.

I will take up the work of this day as a personal Pledge to do my best—with interest and enthusiasm. I will do the things I have failed to do before. I will attempt new things that I know now that I can do. I will go ahead.

I will play the game today with a warm heart and a cool head. I will smile when I feel like frowning. I will be patient when I feel tempted to scold. I will take personal command of myself.

I will be loyal to the concern for which I toil. I will be faithful to all my trusts. I will master the smallest detail. I will boost—not knock. I will do—not intend. I will get things done.

I will work because I like to. I will be fair and just because there is no other way—to Win. I will do right because it is right. I will drink defeat, if it comes at times, as good medicine. I will sweat by courageous effort—determined to succeed at all times.

I will be careful of my Time, considerate of my Health, jealous of my Honor. I will help make this day great for everyone with whom I come in contact. I will work for the people whom I serve with all my heart and with all my mind and with all my strength. For in the glory and success of my concern is hidden the glory and success of my own self.

I will make this day Worth While.

❖❖❖❖

Far better it is to dare mighty things, to win glorious triumphs even though checkered by failure, than to rank with those poor spirits who neither enjoy nor suffer much because they live in the gray twilight that knows neither victory nor defeat.

—Theodore Roosevelt, 1858-1919

Dreams come true when desire transforms them into concrete action. Ask life for great gifts and you encourage life to deliver them to you.

—Napoleon Hill, 1883-1970

Risks are necessary if you are to progress on the journey of success. It is better to risk ten times and finally succeed than never have taken a risk at all.

—Don M. Green, Executive Director
Napoleon Hill Foundation

❖❖❖❖

Grasp your Chances as they come.

For it's the approaching of the Goal—just ahead—the turning of the Chance into Achievement, that stirs and spurs the striving man to the fought-out fact of the thing dreamed about, planned about—and done.

Take advantage of the smallest chance.

First see it. Then grasp it! Then bolt it to your very soul. Remembering that Chances seen—and secured—breed Ideas, mould the Characters of mighty Men—and make Success sure.

Master the trivial. And the big things will loom into Deeds, perfectly plain, exact—undertakable. Especially is this true of the beginner of big things starting small. Deeds done determine the value of the Chance seized by the man.

The large tasks of the world lie hidden underneath the smallest Chances sought for with calm Patience and cool Courage. If past Chances appear neglected, passed by, or not seen, the future Chances streak toward you from in front—or maybe latent—but ready. Seek them, find them. Then hold them—"for keeps."

Success follows the Chances nailed down—things done.

You—today—go after the Chances. Take them, ruddy and new, and build from this day, things worth while and things for more than today.

Grasp your Chances as they come.

❖❖❖❖

The distance doesn't matter, it is only the first step that is difficult.

—Marie de Vichy-Chamrond marquise du Deffand, 1697-1780

Time is a master worker which heals the wounds of defeat and disappointment, rights all wrongs, and turns all mistakes into capital, but it favors only those who kill off procrastination and move toward the attainment of some preconceived objective with Definiteness of Purpose. Second by second, as the clock ticks off the distance, time is running a race with every human being. Delay means defeat, because no one may ever make up a single second of lost time.

Move with decision and promptness and time will favor you. If you hesitate or stand still, time will wipe you off the board. The only way you can save time is to spend it with wisdom.

Tell me how you use your spare time and how you spend your money, and I will tell you where and what you will be ten years from now.

—Napoleon Hill, 1883-1970

❖❖❖❖

PROMPTNESS

Be on Time.

Because of the lateness of Marshal Grouchy of the French army at the battle of Waterloo, Blucher had time to whip his army on to the help of Wellington. Napoleon ordered rightly. Had not the man to whom he entrusted those orders blundered—hesitated—been Late—the whole history of Europe would have been changed from 1815.

Be on Time.

"The Train was late," is the most frequent explanation after a terrible accident. What a multitude of lives have been lost, what an army of men and women have been deprived of position and honor, what untold suffering and humiliation have followed in the path of the late Mr. Late. Nothing pays better than Promptness.

Be on Time.

Promptness is the act of being on the job when your name is called—and answering to it. Not NEARBY—but THERE.

Be on Time.

Time tolls its minutes with even, regular strokes. The Job, the Appointment, the Order, the Friend, the Opportunity—won't wait for the man who doesn't respond on the dot.

Be on Time.

There is no winning to the slothful. The world with all its wonderful offerings gives its Choice freely to the man of his word.

Be on Time.

Be on Time at your desk each day—at each and every Appointment throughout each day. The path to greatness starts by being on time each morning at your own Breakfast table. That's the beginning anyway.

Be on Time.

❖❖❖❖

Losers visualize the penalties of failure. Winners visualize the rewards of success.

—Dr. Rob Gilbert

Autosuggestion is the agency of control through which an individual may voluntarily feed his subconscious mind on thoughts of a creative nature or, by neglect, permit thoughts of a destructive nature to find their way into this rich garden.

—Napoleon Hill, 1883-1970

*Napoleon Hill wrote his classic best seller **Think and Grow Rich** in 1937. The book was a tremendous success. It was printed three times and even then at a high price of $2.50 during the Great Depression. The author wrote that thoughts truly are things. It is first a thought then a thing.*

—Don M. Green, Executive Director
Napoleon Hill Foundation

❖❖❖❖

THOUGHTS

Thoughts are what happen when your Brain gets busy. Also, Thoughts are the Servants sent out by your Mind to shape and complete Deeds.

Feed your Thoughts the right Food.

Thoughts are never inherited. Thoughts are individual and belong wholly to you who create them. So, in turn, you are responsible for them. Care for them with zeal. Keep them Clean and Wholesome.

Feed your Thoughts the right Food.

Thoughts are the Master Builders of Fate. And as sure and plain as the chisel in the hands of the Sculptor leaves the lines and form of the finished Statue, so do Thoughts cut and shape your Character—and no man can change their work. Thoughts are Messengers of Events.

Feed your Thoughts the right Food.

Train your Thoughts. Organize them. Concentrate them. Exercise them. Guard them. Glory in the Society of your Thoughts—alone. For your Thoughts are your best Companions. Besmirch them—betray them, and you loom useless and abandoned.

Feed your Thoughts the right Food.

As your Mind grows in Strength, your Thoughts increase in Power. It is a wise plan, therefore, to fill your Mind with Thoughts that inspire and cheer and ennoble. For in the darker days of stress and rebellion that come into every life, the re-enforcements of great and useful Thoughts, step out to Protect and Save.

❖❖❖❖

Be bold—and mighty forces will come to your aid.

—Basil King

The finest thoughts which will find their way into print in these pages are thoughts which were born of struggle and hardship.

Turn back the pages of history; back to the very beginning of all that we know of civilization, and you will find that the men and women whose names live after they passed on were those whose efforts were born of struggle, hardship and failure.

Men may leave behind them monuments of marble without struggle, hardship and failures, but those who would build monuments in the hearts of their fellowmen, where neither the disintegrating forces of the elements nor the degrading hand of man can destroy them, must pay the price in sacrifice and struggle!

To him that hath it shall be given, and to him that hath not it shall be taken away, even that which he hath.

Nothing more true to human nature was ever said than this. Like attracts like. Wealth attracts wealth and poverty attracts poverty. It is the way of human nature.

—Napoleon Hill, 1883-1970

❖❖❖❖

THE BATTLE

The greatest Battles being fought anywhere are those you fight daily inside your own Soul—against Anger, Lies, Habits, Misjudgments, Ill Health—Circumstances. Continually it is The Battle.

The Battle—to find out how far Brain and Body fiber can be put to the test in order to learn that The Man is in Command.

Heroes pass us daily—and we know it not.

Character and Strength come from Strife. Like the Diamond, you become valuable only after the most painstaking toil and effort. We all come up out of the rough—we all demand cutting and polishing and shaping before we are able to stand out beautiful and inspiring.

But Battling should hold nothing of gloom and sourness. For even in Defeat, there is always something Won. The main requisites are to keep Smile-bound, carry Light Equipment, and in the words of Cromwell, "trust in God and keep your Powder dry."

Welcome The Battle, as it goes on in your life. Plan each little Skirmish with Care and with Courage. Be unmindful of the outside Crowd. Center on the destroying forces that face you and fight them to a finish. Then get ready for another Battle. Charge the dissenters in your own ranks. But keep your face toward the Enemy, under whatever name it fights you.

Always battle to Win!

By firmly and patiently loading and reloading the guns at your command you become a seasoned Soldier. Little by little the intricate rules and principles of warfare become more simple and understandable. You begin to feel yourself a Leader and a Conqueror.

Thus does the Battle—fought out by us hourly with fortitude—make real Men and Women of us all.

❖❖❖❖

*When someone uses the phrase "He (or she) is a **real people person**," the meaning conveyed is that of someone outgoing . . . warm . . . and charming. A **real people person** is one who is able to put others at ease and . . . make them feel important.*

But anyone can be a people person. By this I mean one who puts human concerns first, one who relates to his or her fellow human beings as people, not as fixtures.

Even the most introverted individual can be a people person if he continuously tries and especially if he uses man's greatest power—the power of prayer. It isn't so difficult for extrovert. If you are a people person at heart and act accordingly, others will recognize it.

It is absolutely imperative for leaders, whether they be executives, sales managers, parents or a friend, to aspire to become a true people person. You can become a true people person by developing the habit of a Positive Mental Attitude, known as PMA, in your dealings with others. You will be considerate of them and treat them as you would want to be treated.

—**W. Clement Stone, 1902-2002**

Showing appreciation for others is a great idea that will pay rewards. Doing a good deed is not only the right thing to do but the person showing appreciation to others will feel better about themselves.

Showing appreciation to others can be a simple thank you, a card to someone who has done a good job or been recognized in some manner.

—**Don M. Green, Executive Director**
Napoleon Hill Foundation

❖❖❖❖

APPRECIATION

Appreciation is the Salt that savors the work and life of the World. Without Appreciation for what we do and without Appreciation for what is done for us, the merest task would become a burden and the Sunshine would go down out of the Hearts of People.

Express your Appreciation.

Appreciation is often withheld for fear of an advantage being taken of it. Nothing could be more foolish. Such a man takes advantage of himself. Appreciation acts like oil on the dry, worn parts of a machine. It starts off everybody and everything with Smiles. Continued Appreciation keeps things running smoothly. Also it saves wear.

Express your Appreciation.

People waste away, render but half service, and finally drop back in the race simply through a lack of Appreciation. Appreciation is not only one of the most powerful Tonics on earth—it's an actual necessary Food. And without it no one partakes of a Balanced Diet.

Express your Appreciation.

If you are an Employer and one of your Helpers does good work, tell him so. And if you are a Helper and your Employer encourages you on, tell him so in thanks and increased service. Appreciation stirs and stimulates. It goes to a man's soul as an electric current to the sensitive nerve centers.

Express your Appreciation.

Appreciate the chance to Live. Appreciate your Health, your Home, your Father and Mother, your Friends, your Opportunity. Some of these you may not have. But Appreciate what you do have—and greater gifts will hourly be added.

❖❖❖❖

You do not lead by hitting people over the head. That's assault not leadership.

—Dwight D. Eisenhower, 1890-1969

Optimism is one of the most important traits of a pleasing personality. But it results largely from other traits—a good sense of humor, hopefulness, the ability to overcome fear, contentment, a positive mental attitude, flexibility, enthusiasm, faith, and decisiveness.

Remember that no great leader or successful person was ever a pessimist. What could such a leader promise his followers but despair and defeat? Even in the darkest days of the Civil War, leaders on both sides—such as Abraham Lincoln and Robert E. Lee—held faith in better days to come.

Franklin D. Roosevelt's natural optimism breathed a new spirit of hope into a dejected nation in the depths of the Depression.

Be a Leader—Practice Justice

The first trait of the leader is a willingness to make decisions and accept responsibility for them. The second trait, coupled closely with the first, is a keen sense of justice.

—Napoleon Hill, 1883-1970

Henry Ford said, "If you think you can or think you can't, you are right."

Do not let others determine whether you can or cannot do those things that you have determined to be important in your life.

—Don M. Green, Executive Director
Napoleon Hill Foundation

❖❖❖❖

86

LEAD

This world needs Leaders more than it needs any other breed of men. Every line of activity calls for Leaders—every Home, every Business, every Town—every Nation. As long as there are people there will be plenty to Follow. The demand is for those who can Lead.

Be a Leader.

The greatest asset in Leadership is Courage. Cowards never Lead. Leadership requires great Patience. No one will follow an Irritable or Impatient Leader. Leadership requires Tact, Fairness and Confidence. One man can't Lead another who distrusts his Leadership. Many other things are important—but these things are Imperative.

Be a Leader.

A Leader must inspire and wake up the sleeping POWERS in his followers. He must be able to draw out, into action, the very highest qualities of people. To be able to do this he must himself have a clean consistent Record. A man can't command without Authority—a man can't stir other people without first having stirred himself and become his own Master.

Be a Leader.

It is just as important to be a Leader in your own Home or Town as to be a Leader in your Country. It isn't the special station in which a man Leads that makes his work most important but it's HOW he Leads. This thing is true—that if you Lead well in the little affairs of life you can't keep from becoming a Leader in the big affairs.

Be a Leader.

❖❖❖❖

Vision is the art of seeing things invisible.

—Jonathan Swift, 1667-1745

Creative Vision has its base in the spirit of the universe which expresses itself through the brain of man.

—Napoleon Hill, 1883-1970

Creative Vision extends beyond the interest in material things. It judges the future by the past and concerns itself with the future more than with the past. Imagination is influenced and controlled by the powers of reason and experience. Creative Vision pushes both of these aside and attains its ends by basically new ideas and methods.

Imagination recognizes limitations, handicaps and opposition. Creative Vision rides over these as if they did not exist and arrives at its destination. Imagination is seated in the intellect of man. Creative Vision has its base in the spirit of the universe, which expresses itself through the brain of man. Note well these distinctions if you desire the difference between genius and mediocrity, for genius is the product of Creative Vision, while mediocrity is the product of the imagination, albeit a product that often carries power and attains stupendous ends.

—Napoleon Hill, 1883-1970

❖❖❖❖

VISION

Vision is Act-seeing. Great Vision means that you see things DONE by way of your Imagination, even before they are attempted. Vision differs from Imagination. It starts from Imagination. Imagination takes the Pictures but Vision turns them over to the Architects who Build things from them. Men with Vision are Dominant.

Look Out.

Muster your Ideas. For Ideas germinate Vision. They give it Flesh and Blood, Feed its Fire Box, Control its Nerves—Pump its Heart. Ideas make Vision a living thing.

Look Out.

Despise Vision and you become a Hireling—dependent and owned. Court Vision and you become a Master—a Weilder of Power unlimited. Vision is Optimism with two healthy Eyes.

Look Out.

Vision comes to, and may be gained by, the humblest. It carries neither a Patent nor a Copyright. It's a "tramp" element in the sense of freedom. But it must be sought, found—and then fed and clothed. Vision comes to no one unhunted.

Look Out.

Your Vision is Big or Little as you will it. The greater you aspire the greater will grow your Vision. The farther you See—the more you will Do. Vision is applicable to the everyday. It puts strength back of effort. It brings Permanence to your acts.

Look Out.

❖❖❖❖

True silence is the rest of the mind; it is to the spirit what sleep is to the body, nourishment and refreshment.

—William Penn, 1644-1718

I am convinced that one of the evilest of evils is that of talking too much and listening too little. By tactfully drawing people into conversation, which is by no means a difficult task in most cases, you can find out what is in the mind of another. By keeping your own mouth shut and your ears open you surround yourself with a tremendous advantage over the fellow who talks with unguarded enthusiasm. It is a poor compliment to a man to have it said of him that anyone who will stand and listen may know all that he knows, yet this might be truthfully said of 95 per cent of us.

—Napoleon Hill, 1883-1970

❖❖❖❖

LISTEN

To Listen is to Learn. Doers of large affairs take very little time to talk—but they are always good Listeners. Anyone may secure a liberal education if he will but take the time to Listen. But it is imperative that you—

Absorb what you Learn.

General U. S. Grant was not a brilliant man. He was a failure in Business. But he set out to become Useful. He was gifted with wonderful determination and doggedness. He had Character. And today, high above the waters of the Hudson, alongside the beautiful Riverside Drive in New York, stands Grant's Tomb—mute testimony to the life and work of Grant, as Soldier and President. So wonderful a Listener was he that while President he became known as "The Silent President."

Absorb what you Learn.

To Listen well is a great accomplishment. No one shows his ignorance quicker than the man who persists in talking without saying anything. If you have something to say—say it. If you have nothing to say—Listen.

Absorb what you Learn.

Select the people to whom you Listen. Listen with respect and an open Mind. Give new Ideas, new Theories and new Programs a hospitable reception. Listen well. To you remains the right to reject what you do not want. But always be big enough to Listen. Then—

Absorb what you Listen.

❖❖❖❖

The best-dressed person usually is the one whose clothes and accessories are so well chosen, and the entire ensemble so well harmonized, that the individual does not attract undue attention because of his or her Personal Adornment.

—Napoleon Hill, 1883-1970

How you dress can also have a significant impact on how others perceive you. A good rule of thumb is to be sure you are dressed appropriately for the situation. "Dress casual" may mean jeans and shorts to a group of advertising agency people while the same words mean sports jackets or blazers and trousers at a gathering of attorneys. If you are unsure, ask. Nothing makes you feel more uncomfortable than being over- or under-dressed for the occasion.

The same holds true for work attire. Acceptable dress at one company may be entirely inappropriate for another. If you want to fit into the culture of any organization, observe how the president dresses and follow his or her lead. If he's an entrepreneur who shuns ties and prefers sneakers to wingtips, however, proceed with caution. He may think it's fine for him to dress that way in the office, but it wouldn't work so well for the sales force to dress the same way when making sales calls on conservative companies, and the vice president of finance wouldn't instill much confidence in bankers if he wore jeans instead of pinstripes to a business lunch. The kind of work you do and the type of people you are likely to come in contact with during the normal course of business should also influence your attire. Again, appropriateness is the key.

—W. Clement Stone, 1902-2002

❖❖❖❖

CLOTHES

Note the man taking care as to his Clothes! He shall shake hands heartily with Success and Success shall take him into Partnership. Clothes may not make the man but a man easily makes his Clothes help make him. They will help you to—

Reveal yourself through your Clothes.

First, Clothes give a feeling of Self-respect. Then it is, however, that the sensible man forgets them. But if he doesn't, then they help to unmake him. Clothes-worship discolors Character and takes from it its luster. For Clothes, after all, are mostly for the Mind. Else we could still dress in skins. Clothes are very accurate indicators to the real Character of a man.

Reveal yourself through your Clothes.

You can do so if you let your Clothes be the means and by no means the end. Clothes and mere Style are of two different Tribes. Neatness and Common Sense in Clothes count most. Shakespeare's advice—"As much as thy purse will allow, neat but not gaudy" is difficult to improve upon.

Reveal yourself through your Clothes.

On the other hand, careful Selection in Clothes, so as to mirror your individuality and personality, becomes one of the most forceful means in your power for your growth. Clothes give prestige. They furnish an "entre." The mental effect of the careful, well-dressed man or woman at once is to stimulate, invite and knit with satisfaction. The great point, however, is to so dress that people become at once interested in YOU and not your Clothes.

Reveal yourself through your Clothes.

❖❖❖❖

If you have built castles in the air,
your work need not be lost;
that is where they should be.
Now put the foundations under them.

—Henry David Thoreau, 1817-1862

Personal Initiative is a prominent quality of all successful leadership in every field of endeavor. It heads the list of qualities that a successful leader must possess. Personal initiative, to be effective as a quality of leadership, must be based upon a definite organized plan, inspired by a definite motive and followed through to the end at which it is aimed. An example of Personal Initiative and leadership is Henry J. Kaiser, who, during World War II astounded the entire industrial world by his achievement of speed and efficiency in building ships. His achievements were all the more amazing because he had never built ships before. The secret of his success lies in his leadership ability.

—Napoleon Hill, 1883-1970

❖❖❖❖

God never put Brains into human heads for mere Fixtures. Brains are just like Continents. They were created to be Explored and Used—to be populated with Ideas. But before you start out on your expedition of Exploration, be sure that you—

Get a Viewpoint.

For next to actual Brains to Work with, there is nothing so important as to have an individual Viewpoint. It is everything to a man. From out of it rises the very Image of a man's life Plan and Ideal. Explore.

Get a Viewpoint.

One man gathers together and puts ready for instant use, the thousands upon thousands of words that make up a Language. We can't forget Webster. He shaped and sharpened the tools—and put them in order. Then Emerson came along. Poe arrived. Dickens, MacCaulay, Scott—and scores of others stepped up and delved into the tool chest of Webster. Each with his own Viewpoint shaped a literary Career. Explore. Find out.

Get a Viewpoint.

The whole World is beginning to bare its head to the genius of O. Henry. But marvelous as his words read, they are as nothing to his almost superhuman worked-out Viewpoint. His Pictured People in the cycle of the Humdrum and the Forgotten, will never die until print perishes. He was always Exploring—Exploring.

Get a Viewpoint.

Search, Think, Sacrifice, Study, Travel, Read—get the spirit of Exploration worked into your system. But remember that it is what you GET from Exploring that makes your Expeditions worth while. First—

Get a Viewpoint.

❖❖❖❖

I like the dreams of the future better than the history of the past.

—Thomas Jefferson, 1743-1826

"Success and Failure are in your own mind."

Once you are awakened by this stupendous realization, you will have at your disposal the 12 great riches of life:

1. *A Positive Mental Attitude*
2. *Sound Physical Health*
3. *Harmony in Human Relationships*
4. *Freedom from Fear*
5. *The Hope of Achievement*
6. *The Capacity for Faith*
7. *The Willingness to Share One's Blessings*
8. *A Labor of Love*
9. *An Open Mind to All Subjects*
10. *Self-Discipline*
11. *The Capacity to Understand People*
12. *Financial Security*

—Napoleon Hill, 1883-1970

❖❖❖❖

Put your Dreams to Work.

The right kind of a Dream is the Advance Agent of a Deed. Dreams are Pictures of things in the mind that the man of Initiative works out and completes. The world's Doers have always been Dreamers.

Put your Dreams to Work.

But when you Dream, Dream near home. Castles in Cathey can be of no use to you. Dreaming of your neighbor's nicely piled woodshed doesn't saw up your own wood in your own yard.

Put your Dreams to Work.

Plan out your Dreams. And as you have them index them so that you will know where to find them when you want them. Sandpaper them so that you will see what they are made of more clearly. Get them in both your hands and hold them up squarely in front of your face so that you may get their full measure. Then give them a Pick or a Shovel or a Pen. Get them into Action.

Put your Dreams to Work.

Forget your Dreams of Yesterday. Get your Dreams of Tomorrow into work Today. Then Tomorrow they will have grown into Deeds.

Put your Dreams to Work.

❖❖❖❖

We often pride ourselves on even the most criminal passions, but envy is a time and shamefaced passion we never dare to acknowledge.

—Francois duc de La Rochefoucauld, 1613-1680

It is obvious that those who are filled with malice and envy do not have peace of mind; their malice and envy sour their lives. Failure so often hates the very sight of success. Speaking with successful men, I have noticed they speak in complimentary terms of other men who are succeeding. Their attitude is not one of envy, but of willingness to learn from others. The failure, on the other hand, goes out of his way to find some adverse criticism of the successful person. If he can't find anything doubtful about the way that person does business, then he will pick at some other area. His malice is evident, and so is the sad fact that he not only cannot command what money can buy, but also he cannot attain peace of mind.

—Napoleon Hill, 1883-1970

❖❖❖❖

ENVY

You who read this little talk, have Things locked up in your Brain that nobody else on earth has or ever has had. And you hold the Key, too. Although the Almighty is in a big business, creating millions of Human Beings, year after year, nobody has ever yet discovered a duplicate Human Being. Every Human Being is "original." So, if there is any Envying to be done, let the other fellow do it. YOU—

Be too Big to bother with Envy.

Now, Envy is begrudging some other fellow his Good Fortune. To be Envious is to stagnate your own growth. The Envy that you have for the Winning of somebody else takes away in just that measure Winning on your own part. Envy is Self-robbery.

Be too Big to bother with Envy.

Call to your own mind the Big doers. Are they Envious people? No—they are too Busy to Envy. If they took the time to Envy they could not have used their best abilities to Achieve.

Be too Big to bother with Envy.

You would never Envy if you would but realize the Accumulated Power that comes by profiting from the Success of other people. Be glad of the Big Luck of somebody else. Be wise enough to let its Inspiration lift you up. Individual Success is not stationary. It has no limitations. Congratulate your friend today and he may be put in the position to congratulate you tomorrow and be happy of the chance.

Be too Big to bother with Envy.

❖❖❖❖

Imagination is the key to all of man's achievements, the mainspring of all human endeavor, the secret door to the soul of man. Imagination inspires human endeavor in connection with material things and ideas associated with material things.

Creative Vision extends beyond the interest in material things. It judges the future by the past and concerns itself with the future more than with the past. Imagination is influenced and controlled by the powers of reason and experience. Creative Vision pushes both of these aside and attains its ends by basically new ideas and methods.

Two things are essential, more essential than all others, perhaps, for the unfoldment and the development of Creative Vision. One is a sincere willingness to work and the other is a definite motive which is sufficient to inspire willingness to Go the Extra Mile in a Positive Mental Attitude.

—Napoleon Hill, 1883-1970

Vision helps us to see things as they can be and not as they are. The writers of the Old Testament said, "Without a vision the people perish." While history is important to study, I think Thomas Jefferson's preference of the vision of the future versus the history of the past says to us that where we are going is much more important than where we have been.

—Don M. Green, Executive Director
Napoleon Hill Foundation

❖❖❖❖

SEE

There are two ways of Seeing. One with the Eyes and one with the Mind. Helen Kellar once stated in a public address that there were many people more Blind than she. She was right. The Blind are those who WILL NOT see.

Keep your Eyes and Mind wide Open.

Joseph Pulitzer, the late Blind Editor of the New York World, made his newspaper great not until after he became Blind. Prescott wrote his greatest Histories with Sightless Eyes. P.S. Henson, the great Preacher, with but one Eye, has Seen more and learned more than most people would with a dozen Eyes. The Blind many times See most.

Keep your Eyes and Mind wide Open.

Use your Eyes. See Things. And after you See them, make Friends out of them. No two people See Things exactly the same. Watt saw latent Power in the Steam that came out of his mother's Tea Kettle. Franklin saw another kind of usefulness snapping from the tail of his Kite. The followers of these men saw enough to adapt and force Civilization ahead by scores of years.

Keep your Eyes and Mind wide Open.

Many of the really Big Things in this world have not yet been Seen. You, at your humble task Today, may See some of them, or shadows of them. And if you do, persist in Seeing. There is always this one great way to Learn and Grow—to resolve on Seeing everything that can be Seen. But your Eyes are only half. To See with your Mind is the other half.

Keep your Eyes and Mind wide Open.

❖❖❖❖

Remember, as you appropriate this philosophy for the personal benefits you will gain from those who provided it, that you owe something to those who will follow you. **This nation must go on.** *The American standard of living must be maintained and raised even higher. Our form of democracy must be protected. Our schools and churches must be made secure for the benefit of those who will follow us, just as they have been preserved for us by those who have preceded us.*

—Napoleon Hill, 1883-1970

To live in the United States is a great privilege that was made possible by people fleeing their homelands to seek a better life. Just think a second, when have you seen news where some person has made a homemade boat or risked their life to leave the United States to flee to another country.

—Don M. Green, Executive Director
Napoleon Hill Foundation

❖❖❖❖

U.S.

In the private office of the President of one of the greatest of American concerns are these two letters in big, black type on a framed card—U.S. These letters might stand for a great many things. But this is what they actually abbreviate—Universal Spirit. They also mean to—
Co-operate.

The Universal Spirit makes men Trust each other, makes you want to be Loyal to yourself, to your friends, to your ideals and to your business connections. And, after all, the Universal Spirit is but the great desire to help make things run along smoothly—to get things done without a lot of useless bickering.
Co-operate.

Fear, Friction, Discouragement, Distrust, Disloyalty—each is but the backfiring of a lack of the Universal Spirit. You won't have any strikes in your shop if its motto is the Universal Spirit. To get it, start with the Golden Rule.
Co-operate.

Believe that you have a composite part in what goes to make up the finest part of happiness and you won't need to use the dictionary to define the meaning of the Universal Spirit. It is just to—
Co-operate.

❖❖❖❖

You will find that Mother Nature goes the extra mile in everything that she does. She doesn't create just barely enough of each gene or specie to get by; she produces an over abundance to take care of all emergencies that arise and still have enough left to guarantee the perpetuation of each form of life.

Each spring look at the blooms on the fruit trees. Nature makes allowances for the winds and storms and unusual frosts that may destroy many of the blooms, by having enough blooms left to produce a crop of fruit. Nature Goes the Extra Mile simply by producing an abundance of blooms that attracts the bees. The bees Go the Extra Mile by rendering their services before they are compensated. The result is the production of fruit and the perpetuation of the bees.

—Napoleon Hill, 1883-1970

Almost everybody has problems and tasks which can never be finished today. But if we get busy and attack one thing at a time, we can then take on the next task; and one thing at a time well done, eats into a pile of things waiting for us to do.

—Don M. Green, Executive Director
Napoleon Hill Foundation

❖❖❖❖

THOROUGHNESS

This world is saturated with Human Beings, Jobs, Businesses, works of Art, Enterprises of Machinery—that are ragged and frayed at the edges, so to speak, because somebody is constantly blundering.

Whatever you Do—Do it Well—to the Finish.

Failure starts to germinate when you first begin to slight your work. The slight may be ever so small—but be not deceived—at that point your Success begins to die.

Whatever you Do—Do it Well—to the Finish.

Have Sense and Courage enough to realize that you will make Mistakes right along. The big thing to Master is the Art of Learning from these Mistakes so that you never make the same ones twice. Conquer every Obstacle that gets in front of you. Win and pass on. Be Thorough.

Whatever you Do—Do it Well—to the Finish.

Nothing that is Worth While is unimportant. And nothing that is important can you afford to neglect or do in a slipshod way. The Employer IS an Employer because he was once a good Employee. Thoroughness is at the bottom of Winning. No structure ever stood—built upon half sand and half stone. Be Thorough—stamping daily upon your very Brain, as a Motto, this thought—

Whatever you Do—Do it Well—to the Finish.

❖❖❖❖

THE MIND OF MAN would lead all the other Miracles of Life if they had been described in the order of their importance, because the mind is the instrument through which man relates himself to all things and circumstances that affect or influence his life.

Without doubt the human mind is the most mysterious, the most awe-inspiring product which nature has produced, and at the same time it is the least understood, and the most often abused, of man's profound gifts from the Creator.

All of man's successes and all of his failures and frustrations are the direct result of the manner in which he uses his mind, **or neglects to use it.**

—Napoleon Hill, 1883-1970

Napoleon Hill in his book **You Can Work Your Own Miracles** *wrote that change headed the list of the miracles of life.*

Change is the tool of human progress and provides the highest standard of living the world has ever known.

—Don M. Green, Executive Director
Napoleon Hill Foundation

❖❖❖❖

USE

Use! This is one of the most inspiring little words in all the languages of words. Think of what this great America was before men began to use it! A marvelous area, true, but so unhelpful to mankind. But as soon as Thinking Men came and began to Work its Dirt—a Miracle flashed into the face of a sleepy Old World. For—

Use is Growth.

Hang your arm to your side and let it remain there over a long period and it will wither away. Non-use always means Decay, Starvation—Death.

Use is Growth.

You have a Brain—may be as wonderful and as great as any that ever worked. But unless you set to work the little Cells that ache for something to Do, your whole existence will become but an ordinary affair.

Use is Growth.

Do you realize that Distinction which comes to people is simply a matter of Brain Cell Opportunity worked to a Finish—merely taking advantage of every single Chance for advancement—no matter how small the Chance?

Use is Growth.

Your Minutes Used, your Chances Used, your Legs, Arms, Muscles—every Power of Your Body and Brain USED, means a sweeping toward your Purpose that nothing can stop. Those who use what they have and what they get, are the men and women whose names spot History. Do you want to be Somebody? Well, then, remember this—

Use is Growth.

❖❖❖❖

The way to develop decisiveness is to start right where you are with the very next question you face. Make a decision, make any decision; any decision is better than none.
Start making up your mind.

—Napoleon Hill, 1883-1970

Concentrate your energies toward making a success of one thing at a time. If you have too many irons in the fire at one time, you can find your self unable to perform. Be a specialist and learn to do one thing just a little better than others, and you will get your reward.

**—Don M. Green, Executive Director
Napoleon Hill Foundation**

❖❖❖❖

ENVIRONMENT

Environment is Self Atmosphere. Also, it's the invisible Power of Circumstances that always stays around within call. Which is to say, that Environment is the Servant of every man.

You can BE Somebody right where you are.

Environment is a personal affair. So, if your present Environment hinders you, walk away from it. Hunt out a new Environment. Men and Women who form the habit of getting things done, make their own Environment, hour by hour—day by day.

You can DO Something right where you are.

Bunyan, in Jail, writing the immortal "Pilgrim's Progress"; Milton, blind and domestically all out of kink, penning "Paradise Lost"; John Brown, walking up to the Gallows, smiling, a Prophet of Freedom; Helen Kellar, blind, deaf, dumb, yet the embodiment of Sunshine and Light; these are Masters of Environment!

You can BE Somebody right where you are.

People worth while to this world, make their own Environment so attractive that it draws human beings their way. You, who Employ, surround yourself with Cheerful Workers. You, who are Employed, keep your mind saturated with Cheerful Thoughts. Your Environment is what you choose it to be. Add to your Worth Stature.

You can DO Something right where you are.

❖❖❖❖

A pessimist is one who builds dungeons in the air.

—Walter Winchell, 1897–1972

You can be anything you want to be if only you believe with sufficient conviction and act in accordance with your faith, for whatever your mind can conceive and believe, you can achieve.

Those words have inspired countless readers of **Think and Grow Rich** *to survive episodes of self-doubt or loss of confidence and go forward to great achievement. Perhaps you are among them.*

But picture yourself as a convicted and imprisoned criminal, stripped of your rights as a citizen, looked down upon by your fellow man, separated from family and friends, incapable of helping those who depend on you.

Without power.

What could the words of **Think and Grow Rich** *do to lift you from despair and self-doubt and help you improve your life?*

Thousands of prisoners and former prisoners from across the country can answer that question. They, as well as scores of prison officials and employees, have had their lives altered by a series of lessons based on success principles that have been taught in prisons since the mid-1950s.

—Napoleon Hill, 1883-1970

❖❖❖❖

WORRY

If you realized just what worry is, you would stop using it in your business. For Worry is the name given by the Devil to his choicest brand of smelling salts and the more you get into the habit of using them the more you come to know what Hell is really like. Here's an antidote for Worry—

Smile, Smile, Smile—Smile!

For where Smiles are, Worry is not. Worry is just plain poison. It is the most treacherous of poisons for it not only eats into the finest powers of your mind and life but it spreads and radiates like a contagious disease. Worry can do no harm in the atmosphere of cheer, great faith, hope—Work.

Work, Work, Work—Work.

How useless Worry is—how foolish! Realize but this and you will very soon banish it and forever abhor it. Can you think of a single instance where Worry rendered you a service? Well, then, get rid of it.

Smile, Smile, Smile—Smile!

Worry never did and never will bring anything to pass. It never earned a cent and it never helped a human being. But if you keep busy, if you are continually seeking to render some service, you will never have time nor inclination to Worry.

Work, Work, Work—Work.

❖❖❖❖

There are two ways of spreading light: to be the candle or the mirror that reflects it.

—Edith Wharton, 1862-1937

We all know by now the positive effects that faith in someone's ability can have on that person.

*This phenomenon is known as the **self-fulfilling prophecy**—believing in people, and treating them as if they have great potential, actually improves what they will do.*

Studies indicated adults do better work when their bosses have faith in them.

These findings presume that only the boss sets the self-fulfilling prophecy in motion.

*It is certainly true that if people who're in charge treat **all** those who work for them as they treat those from whom they expect a lot, they will get improved performance.*

—Napoleon Hill, 1883-1970

❖❖❖❖

ENCOURAGEMENT

If you step into some great seat of Power and Plenty, some day, just get into the Habit of Patting people on the back—with a real Pat of Encouragement.

Give away your own Success.

There is nothing in all the world so stimulating as to feel the thrill of Hope coloring the cheek of some fellow to whom you have just given the Grip of Grit.

Give away your own Success.

Even a Race Horse goes better after a pat on the Nose. The Boot Black gives you a better Polish if you remember to Smile while he Shines. Half the wrecks of life are strewn along the Gutter of Failure for no other reason than this—starved for want of Encouragement.

Give away your own Success.

There are no "Favored of Destiny" Successes. The only winners are the Favored of Encouragement. The Smile, the hearty Hand Clasp, the sterling Cheer—the cup of Crystal Water—these are the things that make Men, mould Commerce and start to humming Cities and Nations. If you like to Whistle, teach the art to somebody else who doesn't know how.

Give away your own Success.

And, by the way, it is the greatest Fun in all the world! The next fellow to you right now, whoever you are and wherever you are, is just as Human as you are. Turn your pockets of Encouragement inside out. Keep them empty by giving their contents away—for they will always be full. And, if these little talks help YOU from day to day, get the knowledge to the fellow who wrote them. It will Encourage him.

❖❖❖❖

The best discipline, maybe the only discipline that really works, is self-discipline.

—Walter Kiechel III

There is no such reality as something for nothing. Everything has a price tag on it, and you must be willing to pay the price in full before you get the object of your desire. This price must usually be paid in advance. It is possible to pay it on the installment plan, in easy steps, but the total price must be paid before the object of your desire becomes your own.

Remember to call your plans and major purpose into your conscious mind as often as possible. Eat with them, sleep with them, and take them with you wherever you go. Bear in mind that your subconscious mind can thus be influenced to work for the attainment of your major purpose even while you are asleep. Keep your mind on the things that you want, and off the things that you don't want, until your major purpose becomes a burning desire. Remember: whatever the mind can conceive and believe, it can achieve.

—Napoleon Hill, 1883-1970

❖❖❖❖

WILL

John Stuart Mill once said that "a Character is a completely fashioned Will." Which suggests as the greatest task in life—the training and building of the WILL.

Think, not merely, but ACT the Think.

For that is the only sure way to the educated Will. To act with decision, firmness, and promptness when an Emergency arrives is to feed nourishing food hourly to the Will. The weak Will is the starved Will.

Think, not merely, but ACT the Think.

Note the Strong Man. He sees a thing to do and immediately DOES it. The thing may look trivial. It may even seem the work of some other fellow. But without hesitancy, as though dispute was greater than the task, the Strong Man gets the thing Done—so that he may have Time for other and Bigger things.

Think, not merely, but ACT the Think.

The Tragedy of the ten-dollar-a-week Shop Girl, the fifteen-dollar-a-week Clerk, the out-of-a-job Grown Man, is the Tragedy of an untrained Will. The late E.H. Harriman once said: "I am not a ten per cent man!" Which was his way of saying that he was Master of his own Will and a King among Doers.

Think, not merely, but ACT the Think.

Of all things Today that you should not abandon, are the things you least desire to do. For Will building is to do the menial, if necessary, the hum-drum, maybe. But doing everything to a finish as best you can. Knowing full well that a daily mastery of the Little Things worth while makes easy and natural the doing of the Big Things when they come around.

Think, not merely, but ACT the Think.

❖❖❖❖

Napoleon Hill once wrote, "The man who is on good terms with his own conscience and in harmony with his Creator is always humble, no matter how great the wealth he may have accumulated or how outstanding his personal achievements may be."

The lesson for us is that prestigious titles and positions don't make people succeed—these can easily be taken away. People are sustained throughout their careers by who they are as persons.

—Donald Keough

Never put off until tomorrow what you need and can do today.

Success is measured by the ability to push forward a little each day. Learn to divide each day into proper proportions; get enough sleep; do enough work; get enough rest; make enough happiness for a harmonious day.

—Don M. Green, Executive Director
Napoleon Hill Foundation

❖❖❖❖

HARMONY

Get in Tune!

We learn our greatest Lessons from Nature. At any hour glance at her Wonders—her Grass, Flowers, Trees, Birds, Rocks. What is the most impressive thing about all these things? This—silent Harmony.

Nature wastes nothing. She quarrels with no one. She dissipates not. Her Team Work is perfect. All her Laws mesh in perfect Harmony. There are no discords.

Get in Tune.

Where there is no Harmony, there is no Progress. Elbert Hubbard gave some great advice when he said: "Get in Line or else get Out!" This ought to be the Motto of this Old World to every one of its Men and Women.

Get in Tune.

There is not a man or business that cannot increase its efficiency over and over again by the application of this simple rule of Harmony—cutting out the Discords—getting back into Accord with the Purpose at hand.

Get in Tune.

Think of the lost Energy and lost Life through your failure to keep in Harmony with your best Thinking or with the concern that honors you by employing you. Do you realize that what you are carelessly discarding can never be secured again? Stop—this very minute—the leaking of Smiles, high Purposes, big Resolves. Rebellious Thinking cuts into the Heart of your life Force and drizzles it away.

Wake up! There are no dreary days to the Alert—the Masterful. To you who determine to Win, the story of the Stars and the Planets that do their work in perfect Harmony, is the Inspiration that makes every working minute of Your day Wonderful and Livable!

Get in Tune.

❖❖❖❖

The man who knows the value of dependability in his associates, and refuses to settle for anything less than perfection, is bound to be a success.

Elbert Hubbard, the writer, placed such store on dependability that when Felix Shay applied for a position with him, he gave Shay a unique test. Hubbard instructed Shay to go to the stable, saddle a horse, and lead him around the barn 100 times for exercise. Shay did it without question.

Then Hubbard directed Shay to write a 1,000 word essay on the life and habits of the honey bee. Again, Shay did what he was told without question.

As a result, Shay became one of Hubbard's most trusted associates and remained with him until Hubbard died in the Titanic disaster.

Here is what Hubbard wrote about loyalty and dependability: "If you work for a man, in heaven's name work for him! If he pays you the wages that supply you with your bread and butter, work for him—speak well of him, think well of him, stand by him, and stand by the institution he represents."

There is no substitute for dependability. It is the foundation for trust between a boss and his subordinates, a professional and his clients, a store owner and his customers. It is essential in business and personal relationships.

Notice that the word "depend" comes before "ability" in spelling the word.

Many executives rate the two qualities in that same order in choosing employees for advancement to high positions.

—Napoleon Hill, 1883-1970

❖❖❖❖

ESSENTIALS

Do you want to DOUBLE your Efficiency, your Influence, your Results—your very life? Here's a Secret—cut out the NON-essentials.

Give your Time to Things that Count.

Half the "Faithful" Employees, the "Always-to-be-depended-upon" people that fill the Offices and Shops of the land, are nothing more nor less than just "Putterers," and their Employers are too blind to see it. They do their work from day to day—but they take twice the Time necessary and thus WASTE for their Employers one-half.

Give your Time to Things that Count.

Did you ever watch the Doer, the Executive, the Leader—at his job? He instantly sees the BIG things in his Correspondence; immediately he sees the LARGE side of an Employee or of a Problem. Then he dismisses NON-essentials, and sees that the Essentials are DONE—carried out according to his orders. Such a man is usually the one, too, that does the most and yet always has TIME—for things Worth While.

Give your Time to Things that Count.

Try to pick out the things in your Work Today that really look Essential. Then push aside and away, the useless details. Concentrate on Essentials. For you will never Count in this world unless you—

Give your Time to Things that Count.

❖❖❖❖

The man who does not read good books has no advantage over the man who can't read them.

—Mark Twain, 1835-1910

The mere reading of the words is of no consequence— unless you mix emotion, or feeling with your words. Your subconscious mind recognizes and acts only upon thoughts which have been well-mixed with emotion or feeling.

—Napoleon Hill, 1883-1970

The reading of a good book is an essential part of obtaining success. Study the lives of Lincoln, Jefferson, and other great men and discover their love for books.

The person who reads great books will not only be entertained, but educated to a degree that separates those poor souls who do not read.

—Don M. Green, Executive Director
Napoleon Hill Foundation

❖❖❖❖

BOOKS

Books contain the wisdom—as well as the foolishness of the ages. The greatest thoughts, the deepest experiences, the results of the most profound and prolonged experiments, are all embalmed in books.

Grow useful from Books.

The Character of a man is shown by the Books he selects. The Character of a Nation is largely determined by the Books that its men and women read. The wealth of the world is in the Books, not in its Gold and Silver and precious Stones and Structures and Lands.

Grow useful from Books.

Good books are real. They are cross sections of life. They tell the truth and conceal nothing. You take or leave what such a book teaches. You know, without asking, its true value. You think, act, walk, work—live with it. For the time you are of it—a part. You live over the thought that the writer lived. Though long years in his grave—again he breathes, and warmth is in his blood again. How marvelous is a Book!

Grow useful from Books.

Good Books make sympathy a world trait. Progress is but the accumulation of Book power. With books gone the world would rot away. Good Books will put Poetry and Music into your smallest efforts.

Grow useful from Books.

The world's greatest doers have been the world's greatest readers. "Read again," said Napoleon to an officer on board the ship that was taking him into exile forever, "read again the poets; devour Ossian. Poets lift up the soul, and give to man a colossal greatness."

Grow useful from Books.

Read Good Books regularly and systematically. Learn Books. Love Books. LIVE Books.

❖❖❖❖

- *Some people accumulate money so that they can convert it into happiness, but the wiser ones accumulate happiness so they can give it away and still have it in abundance.*
- *Happiness can be multiplied by sharing it with others without diminishing the original source. It is the one asset which increases when it is given away.*
- *A smile is a little thing that may produce **big results**.*
- *Happiness is found in doing—not merely in possessing.*
- *You can't find happiness by robbing another of it. Ditto for economic security.*
- *A smile helps one's looks and makes him feel better without cost.*
- *Any person can be won by affection quicker than by hatred.*
- *The man who gives freely of happiness always has a big stock of it on hand.*
- *You can laugh off worries that you can't scare off with a frown.*

—Napoleon Hill, 1883-1970

A positive mental attitude is an absolute necessity to a salesman. A negative minded person will find it difficult to sell anything.

A proper mental attitude determines to a large degree the amount of success one obtains. It has been repeated that mental attitude is everything.

—Don M. Green, Executive Director
Napoleon Hill Foundation

❖❖❖❖

122

RADIATE

The most useful body in the heavens is the Sun. It keeps the world out of continual darkness. It Radiates its greatest gift—Light. Also it Radiates its heat—keeps this old Earth warm. Take a lesson from the Sun— Radiate your Influence.

Make it worth Radiating. Radiate it to your Friends. Radiate it to your Office Helpers. Radiate it in your Public Position. Radiate it through your own approval, and take to heart the responsibility that gives you the chance to make your Influence.

Radiate your Smiles.

For Smiles and Cheer are the greatest stimulators in the world. You don't have to speak to Radiate Smiles and Cheer. They shoot their rays of warmth and healing and encouragement from the very lines of your Face and very movements of your body.

Radiate your Knowledge.

Do it to a high purpose. Knowledge kept is of no value whatever. The only Knowledge worth having is what you give away. What Knowledge you get, Radiate.

Radiate your Money.

Earn it honestly and well. Then Radiate it to useful ends. Divide it with the faithful workers who helped you make it. Money is a most useless thing in itself. Its total value lies in what it Radiates in hopeful enterprises and noble works.

Radiate your Success.

There is nothing so stimulating, to a real Winner as to hand out the secrets and formulas of Success that he has learned. Nature works in rotation. So does a man's Success. What is yours today is the other fellow's tomorrow. Your service is to keep the law—to Radiate today what came to you yesterday. For the whole rule of life and Success is to Radiate—To Radiate.

❖❖❖❖

You cannot do a kindness too soon, for you never know how soon it will be too late.

—Ralph Waldo Emerson, 1803-1882

Courtesy is the habit of rendering useful service without the expectation of direct reward, the habit of respecting other people's feelings under all circumstances. It is the habit of going out of one's way, if need be, to help any less fortunate person whenever possible. Last but not least, Common Courtesy is the habit of controlling selfishness and greed, envy and hatred.

—Napoleon Hill, 1883-1970

❖❖❖❖

COURTESY

To some Courtesy may seem a Lost Art, little worth bringing back. But it is not. Courtesy is one of the Old Time Arts that dies only with the Man or the Business. For the rise of many a Man and Business has started with it.

Take time to be Courteous.

Emerson once wrote: "Give a boy address and accomplishments, and you give him the mastery of Palaces and Fortunes wherever he goes." Courtesy is of more value to a man than a thousand letters of written recommendations. Courtesy is an asset of more power than Money or Influence.

Take time to be Courteous.

A few years ago, a young man by the name of Wallace stood behind a Railroad office window in Oil City, Pennsylvania, as a Ticket Agent. But he didn't stay there ALL the time. When he saw a chance to render a Courteous favor by delivering tickets direct to a customer, he delivered the tickets. Also, he sought out new ways of giving service. Business grew. A bigger job came after him. Then a bigger one. Today, still a young man, he is General Passenger Agent for the entire Erie Railroad. He may be its President some day. He owes his career to Courtesy.

Take time to be Courteous.

Courtesy lightens the burdens of toil. Courtesy demands respect. Courtesy is a little brother to Opportunity and follows her around through the hours of the busy day. Courtesy always leads a man higher up.

Take time to be Courteous.

The Courteous Office Boy, the Courteous Clerk, the Courteous Stenographer, the Courteous Manager, the Courteous Leader at heavy tasks—whoever heard of such a one not growing, not climbing into greater things? Think over these truths. For it is tremendously worth while to—

Take time to be Courteous.

❖❖❖❖

In the long run, men hit only what they aim at.

—Henry David Thoreau, 1817-1862

You have a great potential for success, but first you must know your own mind and live your own life—then you will find and enjoy that mighty potential. Become acquainted with your inner self and you can win what you want within a time limit of your own choosing. Certain special techniques help you win the goals of your dearest dreams, and every one of these techniques is easily within your power.

—Napoleon Hill, 1883-1970

We should all realize that definiteness of purpose is the starting point of all achievement. In simple terms how can we expect to reach our goals when we do not possess them. Most people never get to this very important part of success. Failures never decide what they want from life. Knowing what to aim for is a beginning that you cannot skip if you wish to travel the road to success.

—Don M. Green, Executive Director
Napoleon Hill Foundation

❖❖❖❖

AIM

Have a definite purpose—Aim.

The secret of all Winning is the unyielding fight toward a definite Ideal or Plan. A man with a set Aim and the courage to follow in its path cannot Fail. In fact, what you Aim to be, you already are—potentially.

Have a definite purpose—Aim.

The first efforts of John Keats were laughed to scorn by his critics, but he paid no attention to them, for he was certain of his ability and hardly was the ink on their criticisms dry before he handed them his marvelous poem Endymion. "I was never afraid of failure," said he, "for I would sooner fail than not be among the greatest." Keats was but twenty-six years of age when he died—a mere boy! But he had a world fame—he had achieved his Aim.

Have a definite purpose—Aim.

Washington lost more battles than he won. But his Aim for Independence was achieved. People marvel at the election to the Presidency of Woodrow Wilson—a Schoolmaster. But those who know the man, know that he has been preparing for this exalted office for a quarter of a century—not Aiming at the Office merely—but the ability to FILL it. His Aim was to merit the Task—not the Honor alone.

Have a definite purpose—Aim.

There are no "Lucky Dogs." Winners are just the Workers with an Aim—that's all. The Successful business men of every city—the largest number of them—had nothing to begin with but a single Aim. What is their story now? The magnificent blocks, and great enterprises that make each city what it is. Have you an Aim? You only need ONE big central Aim. Get it without delay. Then follow it consistently and courageously. For it is better to Aim at one great task and complete it acceptably and with Honor, than to split your Aims into a dozen different Aims and win in none.

Have a definite purpose—Aim.

❖❖❖❖

Sometimes we need to remind ourselves that thankfulness is indeed a virtue.

—William J. Bennett

The best investment on earth is a courteous, "I thank you." The store that uses it may count upon the customers to return.

Take inventory of people who have succeeded in business, and you will find that those who have succeeded most were those who gave everyone full credit for achievements and expressed appreciation for services rendered.

One of the most successful men in America thanks everyone who calls to see him, from the bill collector on down. He thanks everyone who calls him on the telephone.

This same man, when talking to his wife over the telephone, always says, "Your voice sounds mighty sweet today." Think of the love this wife injects into her work.

When he gets his shoes shined, he never fails to compliment the boy on his excellent workmanship. The look on the boy's face shows that this expression of appreciation urges him to do better work the next time and lightens his load as nothing else would.

The man who expresses his appreciation for work well done profits by comparison and contrast, because most people are not thoughtful enough to do this.

—Napoleon Hill, 1883-1970

❖❖❖❖

THANKS

The Thank habit is one of the best habits that you can form. Think for a moment. Did you ever regret a "Thank you," received from anybody? Did it ever make you feel mean, dissatisfied, out of sorts? Has it ever brought to you a feeling of remorse for service rendered? Alright, then—

Get the Thank habit.

It is not necessary to express in mere words at all times your feelings of Thankfulness. Once get the habit thoroughly and you will LIVE it unconsciously. Thankful men and women show in their very eyes and attitude that they have the habit. It's the most "showy" quality possible. It's contagious, too.

Get the Thank habit.

You meet a gruff, inhuman being. He performs some service as though he were a sort of mechanical device. You Thank him. He at once becomes Human! Thankfulness acts like a powerful stimulant both on yourself and upon other people. It transforms. All days are fine days, all people are square people, all happenings are for the best to the one who has thoroughly mastered the "Thank Habit."

Get the Thank habit.

Get it by always acknowledging a service with a Thank You. If your Clerk, or Waiter, or Secretary, or Partner, or Friend does a service—no matter how small—hand over the Thanks—freely, with a broad, healthy Smile. It's a great investment. The Dividends simply roll back to you.

Get the Thank habit.

❖❖❖❖

Definiteness of Purpose is the starting point of all achievement. Remember this statement. **Definiteness of Purpose is the starting point of all achievement.** *It is a stumbling block to 98 out of every 100 persons because they never really define their goals and start toward them with Definiteness of Purpose. Think it over—98% of the people in the world are drifting aimlessly through life without the slightest idea of the work for which they are fitted. They have no concept whatsoever of even the need for such a thing as a definite objective toward which to strive. This is one of the greatest tragedies of civilization.*

—Napoleon Hill, 1883-1970

❖❖❖❖

Hourly thousands of human wrecks topple heedlessly over the Niagara of a Ragged Point-Of-View, and strew the Rapids of Failure into a pitiful sight. The reason? Rudder out of Setting!

Set YOUR Rudder before Sailing.

The boy in School who has as his end but the fitting of his Lesson to the mere Classroom hour, the Clerk who but dreams of his day as done with the end of his eight hours, the man who measures his Success by the weight of his Dollars—these are but illustrations of the Point-Of-View in Life—turned backward—out of Kink. There is but one way to reach the real Port of real Success and that is to—

Set YOUR Rudder before Sailing.

For a Point-Of-View is just plain Purpose. And there is just one kind of Purpose worth any man's or woman's Salt—the Purpose that tends to some USEFUL end.

Set YOUR Rudder before Sailing.

If you start this day with a healthy Point-Of-View, you will end it a happier, healthier, broader, bigger person. How wonderful, too, the individual effect that a high, square Point-of-View has, not upon yourself alone but on your whole environment. In fact, how it makes Environment!

Set YOUR Rudder before Sailing.

Get the right Point-Of-View upon Life. Then it will permeate your Work—make rich the lives of your Friends and your Achievements, bringing at the same time to you a rounded Success. Search out the proper Point-of-View for each task DAILY. In other words—

Set YOUR Rudder before Sailing.

❖❖❖❖

Well begun is half done.

—Aristotle, 384-322 B.C.

Time is a master worker which heals the wounds of defeat and disappointment, rights all wrongs, and turns all mistakes into capital, but it favors only those who kill off procrastination and move toward the attainment of some preconceived objective with Definiteness of Purpose. Second by second, as the clock ticks off the distance, time is running a race with every human being. Delay means defeat, because no one may ever make up a single second of lost time.

Move with decision and promptness and time will favor you. If you hesitate or stand still, time will wipe you off the board. The only way you can save time is to spend it with wisdom.

Tell me how you use your spare time and how you spend your money, and I will tell you where and what you will be ten years from now.

—Napoleon Hill, 1883-1970

❖❖❖❖

This is the most important day in the history of the world. Because it is the Latest Day—and the only Day of its kind that shall ever dawn again.

There is no Tomorrow—Today.

Worry shall have no part of this day. Disappointment, Fear, Envy, Bitterness, Regret, Anger, Selfishness, and their like—they are of the Past a part. They must have naught of standing or of voice in this Day. For, as already said, THIS Day shall never come around again. Its reception must be Royal and the works in its twenty-four hours must be performed with serious consideration and under the bearing of Responsibility and Appreciation.

There is no Tomorrow—Today.

Your Smile Today will be worth the millions in the Tomorrow. Your Efforts, your Deeds, your Courtesies, your Words, your written Thoughts, your ALL, will count for more Today than all your mapped out plans of twenty years to come.

There is no Tomorrow—Today.

What odds if your ancestors were Monkeys a few years back—so you are a Man today! Whether or not you shall be the Great man or woman ten years from Today shall depend on what manner of acting man or woman you are Today. There are no accidents of Destiny. The Big Thing to be is the Little Thing to do—Today.

There is no Tomorrow—Today.

❖❖❖❖

Manners are the happy way of doing things.

—Ralph Waldo Emerson, 1803-1882

Manners are a sensitive awareness of the feelings of others. If you have that awareness, you have good manners, no matter what fork you use.

—Emily Post, 1872-1960

People of sound character always have the courage to deal directly and openly with others. They do so even though it may, at times, be to their disadvantage. Their greatest compensation, among others, is the ability to maintain a clear conscience.

The English language is replete with words that carry every conceivable shade of meaning; hence, there can be no valid excuse for the common habit of using words that offend the sensibilities of others. Of course, the use of profanity at any time, under any circumstances, is inexcusable.

—Napoleon Hill, 1883-1970

❖❖❖❖

MANNERS

It is inferred that Manners make the Man. No—the Man makes the Manners. For Manners are the Man. And they point the path of Interpretation to a Character as surely as does the weather-vane tell exactly the direction of the wind.

Be your Best Self always.

You enter a car, an office, a home, pace a street. People—your like and image—you meet everywhere. Your Manners in their presence mark your standing and your own enjoyment. Your smile, your graciousness, your courtesy, change the gruff attitude of a clerk or the cold reception of the one you face whether it be for your profit or his.

Be your Best Self always.

"Sir," once said Dr. Johnson, "a man has no more right to say a rude thing to another than to knock him down." The man or woman of Manners is the person of consideration and tact. And nothing but the inbred quality of Manner is genuine. For money or social standing or quick achievement cannot give it.

Be your Best Self always.

Now, Manners are a possession most enviable. Few are born without the possibility of them. A large number who have them hidden away somewhere use them not. To find them out and put them to use and to habit is an event much to be heralded. A better day than this to start could not be found. How about polishing them up at home? How about carrying them as you do your grip or morning paper to your office? How about investing them, as sure dividend bringers, in your office helpers and day associates—from the humblest to the greatest? You can do so if you decide as a settled thing to—

Be your Best Self always.

❖❖❖❖

This above all:
To thine own self, be true,
And it must follow,
As the night the day,
Thoust canst not then be false
To any man.

—William Shakespeare, 1564-1616

In the last analysis, our only freedom is the freedom to discipline ourselves.

—Bernard Baruch, 1870-1965

*No other single requirement for individual success is as important as **self-discipline**. . . . Self-discipline is the tool with which man may harness and direct his inborn emotions in the direction of his choice.*

—Napoleon Hill, 1883-1970

❖❖❖❖

SELF-CONTROL

Self-Control is simply manly Courage fully fit—ready to act calmly in Emergency. It's the Man at the helm in complete Power. Also, Self-Control is the Man Self-Happy because Self-Bossed.

You can Be what you Will, if you Will to Be.

For the intricate Forces of the Brain cluster about each other seeking a Leader. And the Man-power steps out and takes command. First of all, you are what you are. Rude hands never shaped you. Divinity formed you in the raw. Then Divinity must shape you into the Strong. Self-Control is the cornerstone of Divinity.

You can Be what you Will, if you Will to Be.

Rule your own Self and you immediately find yourself in the center of things, for you draw others your way. The great Shop with its thousands of wheels, belts, bolts and screws, all working in the smoothest unison, grips the admiration as its marvelous Power Plant, human-like in perfect Self-Control, produces its completed Machines. But greater are you in your Human Shop, while under absolute Self-Control, you turn out Deeds worthy and unending.

You can Be what you Will, if you Will to Be.

Self-Control must needs be made up of Patience, the ability to keep Still when you feel like Talking right out, and the iron holding down of your own Self for the sake of the Bigger Hours. No man ever won anything without first winning Himself. You are a strong Human bundle of Passion, Red Pepper—and Power. Your Mixing of these things in wise proportion and mastering them will mould you into a sure Success. Try, for—

You can Be what you Will, if you Will to Be

❖❖❖❖

Personal power is acquired through friendly coordination of effort, and in no other way.

—Napoleon Hill, 1883-1970

You have the power of choice. You can, therefore, choose to be highly selective. Remember: as you sow, so shall you reap. Your crop of experiences will be in direct proportion to the quality of the positive or negative seeds of thought you plant in your own mind and the positive or negative actions you take, and the suggestions you give to those whom you wish to influence.

Sow positive self-suggestion seeds to gain the knowledge whereby you develop optimism, altruism, generosity, love, happiness, hope, integrity, courage, good health, high achievement and financial success in the subconscious mind.

—W. Clement Stone, 1902-2002

❖❖❖❖

INFLUENCE

Just as soon as you begin to Think or Do something, you begin to have Influence. Influence is something you can't keep at home. And when it gets away from you, you can never call it back.

Your Influence makes you Something of Somebody else.

Influence has no boundaries. Once, started, though it may seem ever so trifling, yet it may have as its destination the farthermost corners of the Earth. If you would get a conception of Power, realize the Influence of a Strong Man.

It is well to remember that what you have that you can't help but give away is your Influence.

Bear in mind that your Influence is never wholly absorbed, nor does it disappear into Nothingness. It Counts again and again. Influence has no end.

The three greatest objects in life—Friends, Happiness, Success—are each dependent upon proper Influence. So it is good to know that even the humblest person is, after all, master of his own Influence. He can send it out to scatter Sunshine or Shadows. It's his Choice.

A man's greatest Responsibility in this world lies in the way he acquires and gives out—his Influence.

Your Influence today is sure to have a tremendous bearing upon the total work of the world. Your Influence upon other people and the Influence of other people upon you is sure to become a Force and a Factor in the complete work of your day and theirs.

See that your Influence is kept true and wholesome and it will return to refresh you, again and again.

❖❖❖❖

Bring into reality the possibility of the improbable. Say to yourself, as Henry Ford said to his engineers, "Keep working."

—Napoleon Hill, 1883-1970

Picture yourself as an indomitable power filled with positive thinking, and with this Positive Mental Attitude and faith that you are achieving your goals, you are relaxed and confident.

—Napoleon Hill, 1883-1970

Sitting down each evening to compile a to-do list for the next day is a terrific idea. The list ranks each task needed to be done in order of importance. The list reminds us to do the most important item first and so forth. By the use of a to-do list we accomplish more and avoid spending too much time on items of little importance. For example, if we have ten items and complete number eight we probably have accomplished much. But if we skip items one and two and complete the last eight items the day has ended and we have neglected the two most important jobs. Try the to-do list and you should be pleased with your results.

—Don M. Green, Executive Director
Napoleon Hill Foundation

❖❖❖❖

FACE IT

Some people fancy that to Dodge some work that they ought to do is about the easiest possible thing to do. The truth is, however, it is always easier to walk right up to your work and—Face It.

No one but laggards dig up excuses for Dodging what they should Face.

It is unfortunate that the most costly lessons are many times learned late in life. The greatest reason for this is our timidity and cowardice in Facing every problem just as soon as it Faces us. Many a man has evaded a problem in his youth that he could easily have Solved at that time and then gone on, but which he refused to grapple with until compelled to Face It late in life under cover of the bitterest pangs of sorrow and remorse.

It takes greater courage to Decide to do a thing than it does to Do the thing.

Have you a particularly difficult piece of Work to do today? Face It. Have you an Enemy? Face him—and make him your Friend. You feel yourself capable of more important work than you are now doing? Face the new Work, and decide to Master it. Whatever your Problem, Face It—with Courage and without Fear, and with the Calmness that comes to a man when he decides to go ahead according to his Conscience.

Sidestep—Dodge, from nothing. If a thing is worth working out, Face It and Finish it.

❖❖❖❖

If you want a quality, act as if you already had it. Try the "as if" technique.

—William James, 1842-1910

It is a known fact that a prolonged illness often forces one to stop, look, listen and think! Thus, one may discover the approach to an understanding of that small, still voice that speaks from within, and to take inventory of the causes that have led to defeat and failure in the past. The death of a dear friend, spouse, brother, lover, that seemed nothing but privation, somewhat later assumes the aspect of a guide or genius; for it commonly operates revolutions in our way of life, terminates an epoch of infancy or of youth that was waiting to be closed, breaks up unwanted occupation, or a household, or style of living and allows the formation of new ones more friendly to the growth of character.

—Napoleon Hill, 1883-1970

❖❖❖❖

POISE

Poise is a large phase of Success already worked out. For there can be little of Success without Poise. Poise is keeping your head when everybody else loses theirs.

Poise is Power—square jawed and firm set.

When Blame all seems to come your way; when the fingers of Fault-finders all seem centered in front of your face; when Failure after Failure files into your door; when former Friends form into foes; when Clouds creep onward, black and threatening—then's the time for Poise!

Then's the time to face the Crowd and cut the air with your command of Confidence and—Poise.

The Cool heads are the Battle winners.

And you who are ruling and conserving through the art of Poise, you are preserving Peace by being prepared for War.

The Strong Man always Listens—and Thinks. In such an attitude he can consider and weigh with Justice and rare Freedom the most puzzling problems. Poise to such a man is like a Bank full of funds.

Poise put into your Character will balance and proportion it—make it fit and formidable.

How many times you have seen the Man of Action at his desk, calm and collected—with plenty of time for anything important—while about him is confusion and an atmosphere of importance that is, after all, charged with very little importance.

Study out and apply to yourself—Poise. Poise starts when you begin to eliminate Fear and Disorder.

❖❖❖❖

Nothing contributes so much to tranquilizing the mind as a steady purpose—a point on which the soul may fix its intellectual eye.

—Mary Wollstonecraft Shelley, 1797-1851

The successful leader must plan his work, and work his plan. A leader who moves by guesswork, without practical, definite plans is comparable to a ship without a rudder. Sooner or later he will land on the rocks.

—Napoleon Hill, 1883-1970

In reading the Old Testament there is a verse that admonishes us if one is to build a building to first sit down and figure a plan.

Two things can happen when an outcome is desired. First one can wait until the plans seem to be perfect, and the other is to start, once plans have been made. Once into a project it may be discovered that plans are wrong or imperfect. The answer lies in not quitting, provided the purpose is worth while, but in getting new plans, altering the old plans, or seeking help from others.

—Don M. Green, Executive Director
Napoleon Hill Foundation

❖❖❖❖

THINGS TO DO

The people who get the most done—and still seem to have the most time on their hands for other things—are the ones who go at their work from a carefully mapped out plan. For in the end, it's the one who conserves and uses to its full, the 24 hours of Time at his command, that Leads and Rules.

The Successful are they that See and Do—the Unsuccessful are they that See—and do not Do.

Having Things To Do—and doing them according to Plan has produced sufficient Romance in the Business of the World, which if written out, would remain undying in its inspiration to succeeding generations.

A single illustration here. Hugh Chalmers, Office Boy, then Salesman, then Sales Manager, then Vice-President and General Manager, of the National Cash Register Company—later President of a Concern he himself organized and doing business into the millions! Each night Mr. Chalmers' Secretary writes out on a little slip the ten most important Things To Do for the next Day.

Time used in Thinking out things the night before or at the beginning of each day and putting them into logical order for Action is Time invested in advance.

Victor Hugo says: "He who every morning plans the transactions of the day and follows out the plan, carries a thread that will guide him through the labyrinth of the most busy life. The orderly arrangement of his time is like a ray of light which darts itself through all his operations "

❖❖❖❖

In all the history of the world there was never anyone else exactly like you, and in all the infinity of time to come, there will never be another.

You are a very special person! And many struggles took place that had to be successfully concluded in order to produce you. Just think: tens of millions of sperm cells participated in a great battle, yet only one of them won—the one that made you!

*Your genes contain all the hereditary material contributed by your ancestors who survived through countless generations. You were born to be a champion, and no matter what obstacles and difficulties lie in your way, they are not one-tenth so great as the ones that have already been overcome at the moment of your conception. Victory is **built in** to every living person.*

—Napoleon Hill, 1883-1970

❖❖❖❖

ANCESTORS

Are you one of those people who like to putter away valuable time figuring out just how you stand as to Ancestors? The fact is, your Ancestors were what YOU are. Some of the best and worst that have gone before you is now somewhere in you.

The wisest things you can do is to discover the most useful qualities of your Ancestry inside yourself, and begin to weave—from where it left off—greater and bigger things.

Ancestry stock goes up every time you do your work better Today than Yesterday.

A story is told of Ney, one of Napoleon's famous Marshals. At a banquet during the Russian campaign, a brilliant woman had been telling Ney of her wonderful Ancestry, when suddenly she questioned: "By the way, Marshal Ney, who were YOUR Ancestors?" "Madam," answered Ney, "I, myself, am an Ancestor!"

After all, the task of being an Ancestor is mighty serious business. It is enough to put us all on our mettle and make us work to force the Red Blood into our Arteries.

In just the proportion that men and women render Service in this world do they forget their own selfish interest and begin to plan out and deal in "the Futures" of their Race. The man who will but get this truth imbedded into his system cannot fail to be a better Clerk, Lawyer, Business Man, Father—or Citizen. And no woman can take this idea to heart without putting Luster to the important duties of her life.

Ancestors? Why, we are ALL Ancestors!

❖❖❖❖

So you've got a problem? That's good! Why? Because every time you meet a problem and tackle and conquer it with PMA, you become a better, bigger and more successful person.

—Napoleon Hill, 1883-1970

Failure is an accurate measuring device by which an individual may determine his weaknesses; and it provides therefore an opportunity for correcting them. In this sense failure always is a blessing.

Failure usually affects people in one or the other of two ways: It serves only as a challenge to greater effort or it subdues and discourages one from trying again.

The majority of people give up hope and quit at the first signs of failure, even before it overtakes them. And a large percentage of people quit when they are overtaken by a single failure. The potential leader is never subdued by failure, but is always inspired to greater effort by it. Watch your failures and you will learn whether you have potentialities for leadership. Your reaction will give you a dependable clue.

If you can keep on trying after three failures in a given undertaking you may consider yourself a "suspect" as a potential leader in your chosen occupation. **If you can keep on trying after a dozen failures the seed of a genius is germinating within your soul.** *Give it the sunshine of Hope and Faith and watch it grow into great personal achievements.*

—Napoleon Hill, 1883-1970

❖❖❖❖

TOMORROW

To the fellow who never accomplished anything Tomorrow is what happened yesterday, but which he seeks to make happen today.

The thing put off until Tomorrow is rarely done Today.

The great Task FINISHED is always the task done Today, while yet there is Time, while yet there is inclination, while yet there is life and health—while yet there is Chance.

The thing put off until Tomorrow is rarely done Today.

Some of the biggest things ever accomplished were done in a day. Napoleon was banished to a living Hell—on a lonely rock with armed watchers hedged about him—for the simple reason that Blucher decided to do his part with Wellington without any courting with Tomorrow. Tomorrow for Grouchy meant Defeat for Napoleon for Blucher, "made good" Today.

The thing put off until Tomorrow is rarely done Today.

It may be easier to do things Tomorrow than Today, but if you take the Chance, the one best bet is that they won't get done. Money earned Today represents Dividends for you Tomorrow. Work entered into and done Today renders back Ease and Satisfaction Tomorrow. Records made Today, inspire and lead great armies of fighters Tomorrow. But—

The thing put off until Tomorrow is rarely done Today.

❖❖❖❖

The women who make a man's world. *It has been said:
"Behind every man stands a woman."* *This statement is not
100 per cent true; but when you find an instance in which it is
not true, you are well advised to ask:* **Why not?** *You will
occasionally meet some rip-roaring character who says he is
man enough to do without the influence of women, but the
chances are he is not able to get along with women or men
either; or he may have such deep inner doubts of his own
manhood that he overcompensates for his lack.*

*The hunter of prehistoric days who brought back his kill
looked forward to the pride he would take in showing it to his
woman.*

—Napoleon Hill, 1883-1970

*Women no doubt deserve much more credit for a man's
success in life than they usually get.*

*History is full of instances—many of which are well
known—and others that are not.*

*Henry Ford's wife provided the money for him to buy
necessary items when he was developing a carburetor for the
gasoline engine.*

*Andrew Johnson, our seventeenth president, was taught to
read by his wife.* *No doubt Johnson would not have become
President had he not learned to read.*

*Many times, the love of a woman provides the necessary
incentive for a man facing obstacles not to give up.* *No other
encouragement can be greater than that provided by a woman
who cares deeply for someone else.*

—Don M. Green, Executive Director
Napoleon Hill Foundation

❖❖❖❖

FORWARD

This is a talk to Women. Both Unmarried and Married. The theme insures Happiness and Inspiration. It has to do with Advancement. Here it is—

Keep Step.

Keep Step with The Man. For he has mostly secured his Steps to something better from you. Behind the Greatness and Work of every man there has always been the name of some noble woman who was greater than the Deed or Work performed by The Man. The world will always bow its head in reverence at the naming of the Mothers and Wives of the Makers of History.

Keep Step.

The young fellow whose name you hope to link to yours—he is taking his "cue" these days from you. You, who already have him with you—how about it? Is he getting his Steps from you? And are you Keeping Step? If not, start now to—

Keep Step.

A man is as great as the Woman who loves him—makes and wants him to be. A great Man can never be greater than a great woman who helps make him great. Your Power is his. But if you give no Power, his clipped wings make him walk sadly alone. His fight then may become one against the Inevitable.

Keep Step.

As he Learns—you Learn. As he Climbs—you Climb. As he Fights—you Fight. As he Wins—you Win. As long as this world lasts, you, who sometimes think yourself "just a woman" will lead and rule. It's your Kingdom, after all. But in the Home, in Business, and before the eyes of people in Public, this must be your love and your life— with The Man—

Keep Step.

151

❖❖❖❖

Defeat is never the same as failure unless and until it has been accepted as such. "Our strength," said Emerson, "grows out of our weakness. Not until we are pricked and stung and sorely shot at, does it awaken the indignation that arms itself with secret forces. A great person is always willing to be little. Whilst he sits on the cushion of advantages, he goes to sleep. When he is pushed, tormented, defeated, he has a chance to learn something; he has been put on his wits, on his manhood; he has gained facts; learns his ignorance; is cured of the insanity of conceit; he has obtained moderation and real skill."

—Napoleon Hill, 1883-1970

Many people want to quit at the first sign of resistance. The following words from former President Calvin Coolidge explain persistence which we must adapt in order to use obstacles in our paths as stepping stones: "Nothing in the world can take the place of persistence. Talent will not; nothing is more common than unsuccessful men with talent. Genius will not; unrewarded genius is almost a proverb. Education will not; the world is full of educated derelicts. Persistence and determination alone are omnipotent. The slogan 'Press On' has solved and always will solve the problems of the human race."

—Don M. Green, Executive Director
Napoleon Hill Foundation

❖❖❖❖

Back of all the tragedy of Failure there is always the tragic truth of Neglect and Slight—edges left ragged and incomplete.

Finish up as you Go.

A few years ago a young man in a Western College got restless and discouraged. He wanted to leave his course unfinished. He sought the advice of a successful man and this was the advice: "Stick it out. Finish Something. There are too many men now with Ragged Edges crowding the ranks." The young man Finished his College course with honors. Today he is a Leader and a Success.

Finish up as you Go.

Many a man stops work with the clock. He leaves his day's work with Ragged Edges. He is the man who starts his days with Ragged Edges, and finally rounds out an incomplete life.

Finish up as you Go.

There is a satisfaction and a feeling of latent Strength in the breast of a man who Starts a thing—and Finishes it. You will find this true if you do it. The most important task is always the task at hand. Complete it. Make is stand square and clean when you leave it. Look it over. Be sure no Ragged Edges remain.

Finish up as you Go.

Make Thoroughness one of your Masters. Searchingly note the trifles. Get them together and know them. For out of them comes—Perfection.

Finish up as you Go.

❖❖❖❖

It will pay anyone to stand on the sidelines of life and watch himself go by so he may see himself as others see him.

—Napoleon Hill, 1883-1970

The doing, of course, is the big secret. Faith can exist only if it is being used. Just as you cannot develop a muscular arm by disuse, you cannot develop faith by merely talking and thinking about it. Two words are inseparably associated with faith: persistence and action. Faith comes as a result of putting persistent action behind definiteness of purpose. Strong purpose and a sound motive clear the mind of many doubts and fears and other negatives that must be removed to permit faith to operate. When you desire anything and pursue it actively, you will soon find your mind opening automatically for the guidance of faith. Faith without work is dead.

The emergencies of life often bring people to the crossroads where they are forced to choose their direction, one road marked Faith and the other Fear. What is it that causes the vast majority to take the Fear road? The choice hinges upon one's mental attitude. The person who takes the Fear road does so because he has neglected to condition his mind to be positive. What if you have failed in the past, so what? So did Thomas Edison, Henry Ford, the Wright Brothers, Andrew Carnegie, and all other great American leaders. All truly great people have recognized temporary defeat for exactly what it is, a challenge to greater effort, backed by greater faith.

—Napoleon Hill, 1883-1970

❖❖❖❖

154

BYSTANDERS

In Life you are either on the Side Lines or else in the Game. If you are on the Side Lines you are merely watching. You are inactive. You are contributing to your personal pleasure. If you are in the Game you are playing hard, you are getting pleasure and you are rendering Service.

You will always get more pleasure out of the Game if you are a Player instead of a Bystander.

All along the streets of any town or city are lined the Bystanders. Inside the Stores and Offices and Factories are housed the Workers. The Workers are the ones who support the Bystanders.

Let no man do for you what you ought to do for Yourself.

To be the mere title-holder of a Job counts for little. You must be the Job in every sense of the word or else you may be classed with the Bystanders.

The worst thing about the Bystander is that he Contributes neither to himself nor other people—he is a Blank.

The surest law in the world is the Law of Compensation. Its Justice works continually. If you do a Service you get back a Service. If you do Nothing you get back Nothing. Mere existence is not Living.

Into your twenty-four hours put Work and Play and Rest, but at no time be a Bystander.

❖❖❖❖

- *The man who calls on his friends only when he goes after something soon finds himself without friends.*

- *Friends must be grown to order—not taken for granted.*

- *If you wish "acquaintanceship," be rich. If you wish friends, be a friend.*

- *If you must let someone down, be sure it isn't the friend who helped you up when you were down.*

- *A friend is one who knows all about you and still respects you.*

- *Friendship needs frequent expression to remain alive.*

- *Friendship recognizes faults in friends but does not speak of them.*

—Napoleon Hill, 1883-1970

❖❖❖❖

FRIENDS

Friends are essentials. Just as air and food and clothing are essentials. For is not he who has no Friends lacking and lonely and useless? Who ever heard of a useless man having Friends? Like attracts like.

To get a Friend you must be a Friend.

The Friend art is a Heart art—all else cheapens it. He to whom we talk and confide and trust is but another of us transplanted where courage and cheer and kindness is ever alert. We go to our Friend and he lifts us up and we feel him coming back to his own again—in ourselves.

A Friend is a mutual partner with whom we need no signed agreements.

It is said of Carlyle and Tennyson that they would sit for hours together without the passing of a word and then separate. And both inspired and uplifted because of the meeting!

Back of the knowledge that you have a Friend is the secret of your ability to press on and win at your plans.

The glory of Friend joy depends not in numbers. Have but one real Friend—and it is enough! The one that will not refuse to understand you, or protect you, but that through the solid and harsh hour of test, will gladly be the other half of the fight with you.

He is your Friend who brings out of you the best of which you are capable.

The sincerity of Service leads you on—makes each day as certain of Success as though it had already been completed and handed to you. If you are in doubt as to what you ought to be in the world, set yourself to the task of making of yourself a great Friend. Remembering that—

A lifetime is all too short in which to be a Friend and get Friends.

❖❖❖❖

Cultivate only those habits that you are willing should master you.

—Elbert Hubbard, 1856-1915

Habits form a second nature.

—Jean Baptiste Lamarck, 1744-1829

First we form habits, then they form us. Conquer your bad habits, or they'll eventually conquer you.

—Dr. Rob Gilbert

The drifter makes no attempt to discipline or control his thoughts, and he never learns the difference between negative thoughts and positive thoughts. He allows his mind to be occupied with any stray thought which may float into it. People who drift in connection with their thought habits are sure to drift on other subjects as well. A Positive Mental Attitude is the first and the most important of the 12 Great Riches of Life, and cannot be attained by the drifter. It can only be attained by a scrupulous regard for time, through the habit of Self-Discipline. No amount of time devoted to one's occupation can compensate for the benefits of a Positive Mental Attitude, for this is the power which makes the use of time effective and productive.

—Napoleon Hill, 1883-1970

❖❖❖❖

HABIT

Habit is a fixed series of acts. Do a thing once and Tracks are marked. Do a thing twice and a Route is mapped. Do a thing thrice and a Path is blazed.

Do the Right thing over and over again.

From the unconscious wink of the eye to the smooth, unnoticed movements of a million worlds, the law of Habit relentlessly rules its course. All life is but a set of Habits.

Do the Right thing over and over again.

The Pennies saved today make the Nickels in the bank tomorrow. The Nickels in the bank tomorrow spell the Dollars in the bank next year. The Dollars saved, crystallize into the Fortune after the years! Habit either makes or breaks—either leads you up or drags you down.

Do the Right thing over and over again.

If you are Prompt today you will want to be Prompt tomorrow. If you are Square once you will surely seek to be Square again. The fight for a thing Worth While right now cannot help but ease the fight for the thing Worth While later on. It is the law of Habit. And Habit creeps on from the minutest Action repeated over and over again.

Do the Right thing over and over again.

Grow Great off of Habit! There is no other way. Start what you do start—Right. Or else begin all over again. You can fondle the eggs of a Python but you can't play with the Python. You can break the bad habit today, but if you wait until tomorrow the bad Habit will break you.

Do the Right thing over and over again.

❖❖❖❖

Study the eagle with her young. Observe, carefully, the lesson she is teaching them. The mother instinct tells the eagle that she must push her young over the crags and force them to develop SELF-CONFIDENCE before they will ever learn to fly. The eaglets fight and scream and hold on to the nest because they haven't the courage to spread their wings or the knowledge of how to "set their sails" so the wind will carry them on its bosom, out to where there is food.

The eaglets are not unlike some people who never attempt to achieve success because they, too, lack SELF-CONFIDENCE, and if the winds of adversity and misfortune blow them toward the precipice of experience, they scream and hold on to their moorings, just as the eaglets do.

—Napoleon Hill, 1883-1970

❖❖❖❖

YOUR MOTHER

The sweetest word in the Language of Languages is that of—Mother. There is in each letter of this word a wealth of music so Divine—there are vibrating chords of Love so Angelic—that the whole world often pays Homage to Mothers whom it honors.

Nancy Hanks—the Mother of Lincoln; Frances Willard and Jane Addams—Mothers to the Motherless; Queen Victoria—the Mother of a Nation of Mothers.

You—whoever you are—your greatest Asset is your Mother. You—bankrupt, discouraged, failure-riddled, hope-wasted, heart-wrenched, self-estranged—there remains still a Day, glorious in Sunsets for you if you will but get back again, in Thought, or Heart, or Person—to your Mother.

The most wonderful Event in the History of the World was when the first Woman became—a Mother. Human Life has become a beautiful thing because the world has had its Mothers.

The greatest Characters in every community are the Mothers. The greatest community is that which honors its Mothers most. The greatest men in any community are those who render the highest tribute to Motherhood.

No one ever has Surpassed or ever will Surpass the achievement of a Woman when she becomes a Mother.

When did you last write to your Mother? If she has gone from you, how often do you think of her? Do you realize that all you are or ever hope to be, started back into the years when your Mother, her whole being pulsating with Pride, held you tight, and with eyes lustered and watered with Love, watched your very Breath, and kept pace, over the hours, with your faintest Heart Throbs? Think of how, all through those days she wrapped you in her Unselfishness and her Sacrifices.

161

The measure of your Success will be the degree of Honor you pay to your Mother and to Motherhood.

How many indelicate stories would you tell if your Mother could always be present? How many mean and unjust affairs would you bring to pass if you had the eyes of your Mother looking on? Never mind about the "Apron Strings" to be tied to. There always comes a time when there are no "Apron Strings" to be tied to. And then you will long for them to come back.

If ever Failure begins to press; if ever Friends begin to fade away; if ever the grand figure of your Will shall begin to bow its Power—do this—think of your Mother and live up to her ideals of you.

Kiss your Mother as you go into the fight of this day. And at its close fill her furrowed forehead with your Smiles. Ease her Cares. Write to her though business go to Smash. Go and see her often though it takes you across the Globe. Let her Living Presence keep you Courageous. And if she has gone from you let her Memory Guide and Inspire you as once you Guided and Inspired her Faith.

For additional information about Napoleon Hill products, please contact the following locations:

The Napoleon Hill World Learning Center
Purdue University Calumet
2300 173rd Street
Hammond, IN 46323-2094

Judith Williamson, Director
Uriel "Chino" Martinez, Assistant/Graphic Designer

Telephone: 219-989-3173 or 219-989-3166
email: nhf@calumet.purdue.edu

The Napoleon Hill Foundation
University of Virginia-Wise
College Relations Apt. C
1 College Avenue
Wise, VA 24293

Don Green, Executive Director
Annedia Sturgill, Executive Assistant

Telephone: 276-328-6700
email: napoleonhill@uvawise.edu

Website: www.naphill.org